African
Diary

African Diary

MY SEARCH FOR UNDERSTANDING

Helmut Thielicke

WORD BOOKS, PUBLISHER   Waco, Texas

Contents

261.83
T43

Preface

During one winter semester in which I was free from my lectures in Hamburg, my wife and I were invited by Mrs. Liselotte von Rantzau, director of the German Africa Line, to make a voyage by freighter around the coast of Africa. In cabin three of the freighter *Tanganyika* we traveled to East Africa from Antwerp by way of Capetown and the South African harbors—to Dar es Salaam in Tanzania and finally to Mombasa in Kenya. Altogether, with the long overland journeys and excursions into the interior, the number of miles we covered in approximately a quarter of a year easily exceeded the circumference of the earth. Nevertheless, it seems a trifle pretentious if the title indicates I "saw Africa." Despite two earlier trips there, I have really seen only the outer edges—but what edges! In its far-flung, yet confined spaces are packed that variety of crises and climates which today shake the Dark Continent: racial struggles between black and white, conflicts with the colonial past, and, above all, revolutionary outbreaks and struggles for Africa between the great political and ideological systems. This diary seeks to comprehend such of these matters as I encountered.

Thanks go to our hostess, whose providential presence we felt everywhere. The men on the boat, whom we got to know well, and who contributed to the richness of this journey, appear repeatedly in these pages, so that I need not name them here. Our first steward, H. Rade, however, remains so much in the background that I feel it would be unjust not to mention his great contribution to our comfort on this journey. He was a master at filling his sphere of activity with an aura of personal warmth. Neither shall I forget our "little" kitchen boy, Ernst. He expressly asked me, when he saw me writing, to mention him in my book. This I am glad to do: ever since that festive evening when we helped him wash a particularly large assortment of plates and tableware he has been our friend. I can only hope that the reader of this diary will make the same judgment which Ernst made of my dishwashing: he looked at the dishes briefly, said "okay," and put them away without complaint.

South Atlantic Course

In the harbor of Antwerp
October 28
Shortly before departure

We have been here three days. The deck is piled high with auto parts. Even the windows of the dining room are obstructed. I have never seen a freighter so heavily loaded. But everything is ready now. The mountainous stacks are covered with green canvas and lashed down. All day long I have watched with fascination the well-planned and smoothly geared loading operations. What one sees here is a microcosm of man's ceaseless activity, production, transformation, and transport. How many stages of the work process had already been traversed in the production of the steel from which the machine components which now rest hidden in these great boxes were made! The boxes too had to be fabricated, packed, and sent off according to a complicated plan while teletypes ticked away across oceans and continents and made possible the necessary sequences of cooperation. Then other work-teams went into action, arranging the loading of the ship like a general staff, so that no vacant spot now remains and the cargo, equal to some four hundred freight cars, will remain balanced and unshifting under the attack of sea and weather.

What we saw in Antwerp is a virtuosity in loading to be found only among pros. Such easy dexterity is beautiful to see and not without a certain amount of aesthetic charm. The crane operator high above us and the dock workers down below in the hold, or balancing on the crates, almost resemble an orchestra directed by the hand signals of their foreman, who controls the placement of the huge weights of the cargo to a millimeter. And then there is the ingenious simplicity of the fork lifts which shove their steel fingers under the high-stacked crates or planks with gigantic barrels, effortlessly lifting them, moving them, and holding them out for the grasp of the loading crane. The latter, a towering monster controlled with two tiny levers which give its nerve center the necessary impulses to set its manifold and highly modulated movements in motion, is a giant with sensitively groping fingers and an almost elegant adaptability. The machines here are really the extended human ego. One can no more imagine that someone would say or even think, My fork-lift or my crane did this or that; no, it was, and is I. The machine is I; it is my extended self; those are my reduplicated organs.

I sit up on the veranda of the deck while it rains continuously. It is just warm enough. Around me the lights go on. Soon the last lashing down is completed. The families of the crew have already gone. Our very emotional steward obviously took the farewell of his wife and young son very hard. And this scene is repeated year in and year out. It is not an easy lot, and the chief burden falls upon the wives and mothers. On earlier voyages how often have I heard a sailor who had received bad news from his family say, "One should be at home at a time like this!"

Somewhat tensely, the passengers size up one another. On a long trip we are, after all, harnessed together, and the close contact on the freighter makes the enjoyment of the trip very strongly dependent upon our harmony. The first meals in the comfortable dining room, the coffee shared in the smoking salon, and the conversations at the bar give us clues aplenty that we are in luck. All are widely traveled, and some are outright characters; thus we are not going to have to be bothered with small talk or a stuffy atmosphere of boredom. Neither does anyone seem to be burdened with a beastly seriousness. Rather, there will probably be fun and shenanigans. An older Belgian couple impresses us from the start. Every year during the winter months, well prepared by careful study, they travel with a laden caravan into the sunny vastness of Africa, always to new countries far from all tourist routes. Both radiate such trust and goodness that they have been welcomed even at secret tribal festivals and esoteric ceremonies. Their store of exciting anecdotes seems inexhaustible. We shall listen to them for many an evening. Their comical little spaniel accompanies them on all their trips. He is present even here and has already conquered us by storm. Besides his clever tricks, one notices that he always wants his master and mistress together. If he has only one of them, he will not rest until he has fetched the other. They are, for his doggy heart, a single personality: his concept of marriage is truly grand!

October 31
Reformation Day

We are sailing in radiant sunlight which has dispersed the northern fog around the coast of France. This so evident promise of sunny days to come gives wing to our mood. Seasoned Africans speak of the friend-foe relationship to the sun which awaits us on this trip and of which I learned something on my earlier trip to Africa. Now the sun is a friend for whom we yearn, a symbol of light and generative life. Rationally we can understand this, but at the same time we cannot comprehend that soon we shall want to flee from him and that a November's misty rain in Hamburg, transported for half an hour into equatorial zones, would bring us indescribable refreshment.

Man, as certainly the most adaptable of creatures, has a high place in the scale of nature. For just that reason, it is good for him to be reminded of his creaturely beginnings, to sense how the ties to his environment still influence him, how his native temperatures and instincts and the accustomed rhythm of the seasons never quite lose their grasp on him, and how each person has his own very special climate. In contrast to the sweeping stratosphere clippers, the friendly atmosphere of our ship allows us to make transitions gradually and to glide through the changes of the zones as if in a dream.

Today I was to speak in Stuttgart, tomorrow in Munich for Reformation Day. Both speeches had to be cancelled because of the early departure of our ship. But at least my thoughts are with those people who are gathering today. The consciousness of this day causes me, as on any larger trip which opens the door to meditation, to begin with a reading of the Book of Job. In the infinity of its inner structure, this story of God opens up new dimensions for me every time I read it. Shall I ever sound it out? While one feels free from all burdensome detail in this expanse, where nothing but water is to be seen from horizon to horizon, Job holds one to the world of man and its doubtfulness but at the same time gives perspective through the depths of its sentiments. To the objectivity which relaxation bestows it adds a feeling of withdrawal into peace. But there is something else which makes me reach for Job again and again on ocean journeys: the greatness and transparency of nature evoked by the majestic images of its poetry. The meditative school into which this leads instructs us never again to relate purely aesthetically to the wild play of the elements or the splendid orgy of color in a sunset.

At sea
Sunday, November 1

Whitecaps glisten in the sunlight. The ancient play of surging waves again draws me under its spell with the magic of its primordial power. In its boundlessness it is not without demonic elements.

Our relationship to the elements has changed essentially. Earlier we struggled against them. They were considered, like the *stoicheia* of the Letter to the Colossians, to be hostile powers, and in myth they often bore the names of rebellious Titans. As

12

powers of chaos, they were to be overcome. Now, however, one flees to the realms of these elements: to gigantic waterfalls; to the thundering impact of foaming breakers on the beaches; to irresistible storms; to empty deserts hostile to life; to inaccessible mountain peaks towering high above the friendly climate; to raging fires in the forests and to steppes which scorn all the refinements of technology. These are the expressions of primitive ferocity which our fantasy crowns with the halo of Romanticism, and whose image we follow fascinatedly on our television screens. Did I look forward to this trip because I would once again be near the ocean elements and, later, to the wild and ancient continent of Africa? Whence comes this metamorphosis which has changed the unbridled elements from hostile into friendly powers from which we hope to gain restoration of health and new creative impulses?

This question also concerns me as a theologian because it indicates a transformation which has contributed to our relationship with the ground principles of life. A negative factor at work here is a certain disgust with civilization: we flee from the "secondary systems," from everything manipulated and artificial, from all the indirect things isolated by the hand of man, back to the basic reserves from which we come and which have not yet been smudged by the fingerprint of a human hand. Behind this escape to the elemental does there not lie a vexation with mankind, an instinct for the fact that man, as a cosmic engineer, has not only made the wild datum of nature arable but has spoiled it; that he has not only exalted but also emasculated, enervated, and drained himself? Does one not suddenly begin to tremble at the possibilities of air and water pollution—those awful by-products of the technological domination of nature which threaten to decimate our environment? Surely man was commissioned at his creation to rule the earth. And that, of course, means nothing more than the refusal to accept nature as it is, and the resolution to intervene to change it and to humanize it. Was this commission overfulfilled in our technical civilization and thereby changed to a curse? Or has this commission perhaps really been falsely fulfilled, with promethean hostility, and therefore not really fulfilled at all? Obviously man carries his ambiguousness with him into all realms which he conquers. And as in Durrenmatt's play *Mission Vega* he will also take it with him to the stars on his cosmic odysseys. He has the Fall at his back, and now Cain will always be present. Just as the Doric columns did not come into being without the labor of the slaves of antiquity, so the miracle of that which we call "modern culture" is not conceivable without the labor of domestic and foreign workers. Man has the distinction of being an ambassador on the highest mission, but at the same time he betrays his trust. Knowledge of this failing could protect against Utopian reveries which dare to drivel about coming paradises and which consider man's present condition surpassable. Man is at all events not only the crown of creation but also its foreign body. This is the basis of his ambiguity, and it is this which causes the psalmist, at the end of his glowing hymn of creation in which are extolled wind and flames, mountains and seas, seed and harvest, to break out in the remarkable expression: "And sinners shall pass away from the earth" (Ps. 104). Man as mischief-maker and foreign body—that is a view of anthropology without which we would fall prey to the worst illusions, and which at the same time would plunge us into despair, if it were the only thing one had to say about man.

At sea
November 2

In the afternoon to port the giant Gran Canaria mountain range which stands out impressively on the radar screen. Memories of sunny days in Las Palmas.

In the evening a balmy summer night, refreshments and lively chatting in the arbor. The misty November of home still lies so near to us that it would not seem inconceivable to see it move across the softness of this moonlit sea.

14

This evening we are to be at the summit of Dakar. We drift in the warm tradewind as the sun blazes, a festival of light. Whales play about us and spray fountains which fall back into the sea in veils of sparkling drops. With Africa still a long way off, we are absorbed in the fulfilled moment. What lies behind us is far away; only the nearest people are in our thoughts. The coming goals are all the more distant because I have no duties which force me to hurry ahead of the moment with planning. I even try not to imagine what is awaiting us because I want to be surprised. It is nice to know that we are being expected everywhere and will be helped in searching out the right places. So let this lovely moment tarry awhile.

Yesterday evening with the captain, Chief D., the chief engineer, and his young wife, a penetrating discussion developed concerning the East-West question and the social crisis as expressed in student unrest. The conversation suggests a good prognosis for our further journey together. Captain U. is universally cultured and extremely kind and considerate. (The shape of his head had already convinced me of his good Swabian background.) When it then turns out that he is from Ravensburg in the Bodensee area where I spent two years of my banishment during the Third Reich, sympathetic threads bind us even closer. The chief is a thoughtful person who, in addition to his technical education, has, as a self-taught man, also acquired astonishing zoological and anthropological knowledge by observation and reading. He is a man who uses his free time on board intelligently, not least of all in making his films, and he is full of plans for African expeditions. The two women also become friends immediately. The rooms of the chief, where we are certain to be spending quite a bit of time in the future, offer an especially cozy domestic atmosphere. Not only does one sense the hand of the housewife on this man's ship but also her desire to keep a home atmosphere for their young daughter, eleven-year-old "Sprat," who is along with them. After many long separations the sharing of such an extended family trip means a great deal to them.

Still later a long time is spent under the sky, which is crowded with distant stars. Whitecaps shimmer with a suggestion of phosphorescence. From the peaceful domain of the ship, this oasis of humanity, we peer out upon the elements and realize we would be at their mercy without our island of safety. "The starry sky above us and the moral law within us"—so we float here upon this infinity. Yet we are more than particles of dust, influenced by elements and stars which travel their paths according to the laws of necessity. We are creatures to whom is entrusted a self-determination which is to be used and yet which also could be our ruin. We are blessed with a freedom which can spoil in our hands and plunge us into a bondage different from and worse than the bondage of natural law which rules the sun, the moon, and the stars.

And yet it is difficult, in this evening of peace upon the water, to imagine an all-devouring watery wilderness, a superpower of the elements. Probably this results from the fact that our fantasy has experienced an extraordinary extension through the phenomenon of space travel. The boundless emptiness of space, the loneliness of the universe plunged in unearthly cold, embraced by the deadly waves of the radiation belt, within a vacuum which would explode our unprotected physical being into nothingness: *that* is the really chaotic power; *that* is the truly fatal element. This ocean upon which we now float, however, is a part of that earth which the Creator has made for the purpose of alloting to us an island of life and safety in the wilderness of infinitude. Of course, chaos also threatens here, and even the ancient conception of the creation speaks of the "water under the firmament and the water above the firmament," of oceans which are withheld from us, whose deadly invasion and deluge is prevented by grace. As signs of a distant power, elemental catastrophes break in upon us again and again: typhoons and boiling oceans, terrestial quakes and floods, famines and epidemics. And yet, compared with the cosmic threat, all of these are only trace elements of that chaos which marks all the more clearly the area of our protection. For this our world—and this is the point of the creation —is capable of being humanized; it gives peace. There are, as Paul said, powers that prevent, that hold back the outbreak of chaos.

In the distance the lights of faraway fishing boats. The men working there lead a difficult existence, and the idyllic appearance of their lights is deceiving. And yet these lights are a fraternal sign. Real chaos is to be found elsewhere. I consider how, at this time, in other places, there is death and massacre, villainy, despair and hate. I think how, far away from this healthy ozone which surrounds us, the air is tainted and the waters polluted. How remarkable is the history of man's dealings with the elements. After he made the deserts fruitful, conquered the oceans and prevented the plagues (I am reminded now of the chorus from Sophocles' *Antigone*), he replaced the aggressive destruction of the elements with a new form of destruction he had himself mobilized against the elements. If earlier he was threatened only by death, now he is threatened by the specter of the population explosion, the super-abundance of that life which his skill has snatched from death. And now the strategists of medicine scheme to erect dams against the flood which they themselves have loosed. If we have subjugated the earth with our culture and civilization, we have also at the same time poisoned the earth, its air, its waters, and its organisms, and are threatened with suffocation by that which before seemed to lead us to freedom.

"The desert increases—woe to him who hides deserts in himself." Man enters the desert not only as redeemer but also as its representative and emissary. "The great Babylon is only a jest, even if it seriously means to be so great and measureless as our Babylonian heart" (Francis Thompson).

17

Yesterday evening the lights of Dakar. Widely scattered fleets, among them a large ship which serves as a factory for processing fish. Very hot. The air conditioner inside the ship is a blessing which I am enjoying for the first time in my voyages. Under the arcade of the deck it is almost unbearable. The air stays hot and heavy. While only a few days ago we wanted an infrared lamp for the arcade in order "to be able to sit outdoors a little," now we long for an electric fan. Our native November, of which the newspapers on board report, is now just as inconceivable as was previously the prospect of traveling out of rain and damp coolness, beyond all seasons, into the heat of the African summer.

For reading I have taken a few volumes of sea stories out of the ship's library in order to get myself in the mood for the voyage. But it appears I have chosen somewhat mediocre things. In the description of ship sinkings (a large number are collected in one volume) even a mediocre writer can create interest, just as in the sexual act, the representation of which does not have to be particularly skillful to engage the reader. (It seems that the only requirement to be successful in this area is formerly to have been a good housewife.) How I would like to have some volumes of Joseph Conrad now, or one of the most beautiful or least-known of sailing books which I read again every year: Ernst Römers' *The Wind Blows Anew!*

Despite the modesty of the literary level, I constantly notice that my intellectual organs of perception are appealed to in theological categories. I seem always ready to observe marginal circumstances: How does man behave in the face of death, for example, a wreck at sea which one will not survive? How do attraction and repulsion, love and hate, develop in the small, narrow world of a fishing boat, diminished in scale, but emotionally intensified? Man always accompanies himself, even if he flies with the wings of the dawn to the furthest seas. And just as he is bound to his identity in changes of scene, so, also, in changes of times. To be sure, mankind progresses, as Goethe says, but man always remains the same. Being conservative probably means nothing other than being aware of this identity in changes of situations and in the midst of all changes. But the opposite is also true: being conservative means, at the same time, the knowledge that this identity of man never exists in static petrification and traditionless uniformity; that it rather hides itself behind mutations and sudden transitions of all kinds. Concealed in picture-puzzles, it must be sought anew again and again. The reactionary as well as the Utopian ignores this. The reactionary does so in that he considers a certain historical condition, in which he lives, and which does not all too greatly contradict his interests, to be the definitive status of history. He cannot imagine that the monarchy which rules him, or the liberal democracy which protects him, or the capitalistic system which secures his standard of living, can be changed or surpassed. The progressive and the Utopian, on the other hand, dream that man can exceed himself, that he can break out of the container of his identity and ascend to higher forms of himself. The reactionary disregards the creation, which remains active in ever-renewing issue, and makes the future a time of surprise. The Utopian, however, disregards the fall of man, which binds man firmly to himself and prevents escape from his greatness and his misery. Man *always* has the Fall at his back—thus the unfortunate term "original sin"!—and so will neither be able to change the world back into a paradise nor himself into a paradisical inhabitant of an unscathed world.

My reading also includes a monograph concerning the "Magus of the North," Johann Georg Hamann. Once again I see that I, as a theologian, have mostly *non*theological books. Theological authors are, unfortunately, all too often people who succeed in writing about the most exciting things in tedious and flaccid prose. I often ask myself whether the people who are afflicted by this verbal anemia have ever experienced the urgent reality of those things of which they speak. It is an embarrassment for my field that, of all people, Dorothy Sayers in her pithy study "The Greatest Drama of All Times" has been able to depict the excitement of Christian salvation in a few pages which, while leaving out nothing essential and even penetrating into the sublime regions of dogma, take away the reader's breath. The so-called progressive theologians who attempt to create excitement in order to find a bridge to their contemporaries, and for whom no fashionable sociological prattle is too banal so long as it bears the banner of timeliness, create only boredom and waste. One does not wish to learn from a theologian what everyone already knows and is already saying. Those who like to trade in the latest and the most progressive will prefer to purchase them without the unfamiliar, and also superfluous, Christian wrappings.

Crossing the equator

At sea
November 9

The long shadow of the ceremony for the first crossing of the equatorial line was seen for a day in advance. The old hands of the crew who already had this ceremony behind them retired again and again to various meetings for consultations. There was even a lady's branch which consisted of the woman radio operator and the two stewardesses. On the preceding evening Triton, the "Admiral of Neptune," bearded, hung with algae, and obviously just ascended from the ocean deeps, came with his train to each mess. There from a large tablet fashioned in medieval style he read the traditional proclamation of Neptune that the inhabitants of the northern hemisphere were to be baptized if he, Neptune, were to accompany the ship any further with his favor. The northern re-

20

gion, he said, was occupied by grimy continents, while in the South the purity of clean oceans predominated. Therefore, those born in the filth of the North required purification at the equator before they could be considered worthy to enter the yet unblemished zones of the God of the Oceans.

An evident nervousness which seeks to hide behind unmannerly jests is to be noticed among the candidates for baptism. There are some feminine representatives among them, including the wife of the chief and little "Sprat." It has been promised that they and some older passengers will be treated gently, although the ancient rules will be adhered to, and things certainly will not be done in the finical and bourgeois manner of musical steamers.

The preparations themselves resemble the construction of medieval chambers of horror. A cube of canvas approximately twenty meters long is set up. The candidates must crawl through it, a process made difficult by the fact that those on the outside continually try to prevent them from doing so. And then they come to an instrument of torture, into which their arms and heads are firmly secured so they can no longer protect themselves. Behind them is the baptismal pulpit, and next to it the throne of Poseidon and Thetis. At the end awaits the "baptismal font," made of boards and covered with plastic.

First there is a great entrance of gods and men: Poseidon and Thetis in Olympian splendor, the baptizer stylized as pope and pacing with dignity, and finally, dressed ready to perform an operation, the physician, with his helpers and several bailiffs.

The young sailors who are candidates have to endure, in addition to the tropical heat, a steam bath together in a tiny room in which the heat has been turned on. Then if they are lucky enough to reach the end of the long dark tube despite the hindrances and torments of unseen foes, they must defend themselves against the stocks. With some of the athletically built ones who are obviously determined to defend the paganism of the northern hemisphere, there are turbulent brawls with the bailiffs. Vocally, at least, the spectators become as involved as at the high points of a soccer match. When the candidates are finally overpowered and firmly pinioned down, blows from a sponge hammer—which looks much more dangerous than it is—whiz down upon them. As they are force-fed sharply spiced "pralines," they are asked how many cases of drinks they want to donate to the present company, that amount having previously been computed according to the wages of the individual. Stinginess and reluctance receive fearful punishment. Anyone who remains immovable is made generous by repeated duckings in the baptismal font. It is astonishing that the most intractible rowdies often become rather quickly pliant, while one quiet fellow cannot be persuaded to donate more than a single case. Physician, bailiffs and baptismal aides, exhausted, finally give up on him. From that time on he is followed by respectful glances whenever he goes on deck.

At the end, each candidate must kiss the foot of Thetis, which is so thickly smeared with soft soap that one finally arises with lathered eyelids and nostrils. There are many accompanying scenes and interspersed episodes, of course, but the retelling of them is as insipid as the description of a wild party. It was interesting for the spectators to discover many nuances in the methods of treatment: the personalities were known and each was obviously given a special diagnosis and therapy.

Some of us older ones, it must be mentioned, had to struggle for a time with our scruples. We were not as naïve and unselfconscious as the boys, and, as we later discussed, we were oppressed by certain concentration-camp remembrances. Although we were amused and laughed loudly with the others, there were nevertheless certain undercurrents of feeling which we could not quite suppress. Just a little bit more, just a little more serious, just a little more evil, and the apocalypse begins. . . . That which wanted to press forward from the background was again and again outweighed by the grotesquery of the moment and by the humor of the accompanying comments. But the rumbling of the soul in the background heightened the critical vigilance of our observation: are moods of brutality, enjoyment of aggression and sadistic urges evident here? I observed the facial expressions and the gestures of actors and onlookers very closely. But I saw nothing unfathomable, only the coarse gaiety that has suited such companions from time immemorial and is long-lost to us over-bred intellectuals. And although one had to pass through severe trials and was also somewhat exhausted after the tortures, there were obviously no residues of revengefulness, no resentment, and no offense taken. All knew that it was "play" and had not been without curiosity to learn what kind of tensile strength they had.

Thus in the evening, everyone from the captain to the cabin boy takes part in a light-hearted celebration: an open refreshment bar off deck and charcoal fires upon which the cook broils splendid steaks. We passengers sit interspersed among the crew. The perfect temperature, the soft evening breeze, and all the good things to eat and drink, give us, after the excitements of the day, a gaiety like that of the Olympian gods in the balmy November night.

At sea
November 10

Since yesterday, noticeably cooler. Pullovers that have been stored away are brought out. We are obviously nearing the South Pole! How sensitive to and dependent upon temperature is this creature, man! It occurs to me, by the way, that in contrast to my voyage to the Far East, no real communication with the crew seems likely to arise this time. At that time we sat on deck together almost every evening and told stories. I very much enjoyed coming together with men of a quite different sort, becoming familiar with their needs and sharing their cheerfulness. I am sorry the reserve is greater this time. One says hello, makes a couple of remarks about the heat and cold, or about the play of the whales, and that is all. I ask myself whether the age difference, which is greater this time, is to blame for this lack of communication. But finally, I come upon a much simpler explanation: On the previous journey the heat drove us up on the deck in the evening so that we immediately formed conversational groups, and we often made our beds in the same hatchway, where we chatted until we fell asleep. This ship, however, is air-conditioned. As soon as we encounter tropical heat and humidity, everyone immediately flees from the deck and retires to the cooled inner rooms. Thus the individual groups remain more to themselves. The technique of temperature control has given rise to completely new social problems. Technology has penetrated even into the sociological structure of the ship.

Afternoons now I spend reading the great biography of Marlborough by Churchill. This thorough work is just right for a voyage because one can stay busy with it. And once again, as so often before, I enjoy Churchill's colorful, subtle style—his dynamic, subjective and highly partisan skill of portrayal; his biased, committed manner of writing history; and at the same time, his endeavor to be fair, which involves the lawyer and the judge in him in permanent and very delightful conflict. And again, I observe what fascination is exercised upon me by certain authors who are doers and writers in one and who experience the tension between the roles of actor and spectator. Besides Churchill, I think above all of Colonel Lawrence, Saint-Exupéry and Ernst Jünger. I must always have one of them with me when I am confronted with the greatness of nature for a long period of time. It is interesting, besides, to see what sort of literature holds good in such situations, or what begins to taste flat and fails. Much of the moderns one consumed at home from cultural zeal goes against the grain here.

Republic of South Africa

After a rich, dreamlike captain's dinner at which our ambitious young cook unfolded his art in all its variety and we said goodbye to some of our fellow passengers, we landed in Capetown early on the day before yesterday. For me it was a happy reunion with a city which I would consider, along with Rio de Janeiro, San Francisco, and Hong Kong, among the most beautiful of the world. The morning entrance into the harbor of a vernal land, the grandiose scene of the city dominated by the powerful form of Table Mountain, made us feel as though we were going in solemn procession to a great feast. As creatures who had been consigned for sixteen days to the moist element and had lived upon a rolling deck, we were particularly receptive to the stony representation of terra firma which rises here in towering formations and yet gives such great room for the settlements of man.

We have scarcely put to shore when the ceremonies of arrival and farewell are celebrated. The ship is infiltrated by an invasion of agents, officials, and controllers of all sorts, while outside an army of black dock workers is already waiting to fling itself upon our cargo immediately. Although it is Sunday morning, the dock work continues undiminished and will go on through the night. Since the harbor, as is the case everywhere in South Africa, is well organized and equipped with every technical implement, we will probably remain here only two days.

How remarkable are these harbor farewells! We had just seemed to be in the intimate sphere of a newly formed family. New friendships had come into being. It was almost as if we had always known one another, for the evening hours of story-telling and strolling on deck had also made us familiar with the life-stories of the others. One first becomes close to another when he not only experiences him in the present time but sees his past with him and can understand what has imprinted his personality. And now all that is dispersed. Suddenly, there are glass shields of estrangement between us. Those who are leaving have now turned themselves toward new destinations and the people who await them. Suddenly, we have become the past for one another. The Belgian couple with their camping trailer and dog has suddenly disappeared. We were so close, and now we have even neglected to say goodbye.

But now we also are surrounded by the friends whom I came to know more than a decade ago on my first African journey. The German Pastor D. comes on board to invite me to speak at a hastily improvised evening with his congregation, and on the next morning at a meeting of pastors.

After a short interim stay in the comfortable, prosperous house of the family A. and a cordial exchange of greetings with their African servant whom I recognized again immediately, a wish is fulfilled which I have treasured in secret during the entire journey: to drive once again to the Cape on the "Dream Street of the World" and to show it to my wife. This is the queen of all the roads which I have traveled. Others "lead to" splendors of the earth. This one, however, is formed by a cordon of them, and one is conducted as through an intoxicating festival. Two factors remain constant amid the unimaginable change of panoramas, the ever-varying bays, mountains, forests, and canyons: the two oceans along the coasts of which this street of all streets leads.

Shortly before reaching the Cape of Good Hope, we drive into a game preserve which is, however, probably essentially more civilized than the planned zoos in the wilder parts of Africa. While we consume sole in a nice restaurant, we observe grazing ostriches through the large windows. If only I could see one hiding his head in the sand! Apparently, the myth attributes to them a vice which is only to be found in man. Driving further, we happen upon a large group of baboons which gambol around and upon the cars. Their animal opportunism, used by these ridiculous white-faced creatures to satisfy their hunger, is obviously stronger than the contempt for man which I, at least, presume they have. Our simian double exerts an irresistible fascination for us. It is probably the magic of caricature in which one sees himself disfigured but in which one must at the same time recognize something we have only seemingly grown beyond. Our children break out in cries of delight at the baboon mothers, some of whom have their young ones hanging under the belly, some riding elegantly upon the back. When we proffer them food, a wild wrangle breaks out over it and there are real monkey dances on the roofs, hoods, and fenders. All this is accompanied by a wild screaming, which often seems a case of everyone against everyone—until the large chief ape comes. With snarling, threatening grimaces, and a chilling scream that even one uninitiated in the language of apes recognizes immediately in its categorical tone of command, he restores peace, order, and fair distribution. "Fair" to him means above all that he will get the best morsel. Here in the ape world authoritarian structures prevail and seem to work well. Democracy would probably be too much for baboons. They cannot even count, and that is, of course, basic to democracy! Even for *Homo sapiens*, democracy is often all too difficult, above all when he believes that the mastery of the simple multiplication table and the counting of votes are enough for his form of government.

We ascend the furthest (if not the most southern geographically) point of Africa and look upon the Cape of Good Hope.

Here historical recollections involuntarily arise, above all of the bold pioneers who crossed these perilous waters and, from this point, set foot upon the unknown continent.

Again I am visited by the remarkable sensation which came over me more than a year ago when we stood at the northernmost point of Jutland near Skagen in Denmark where Kattegat and Skagerrak flow together. Even the powerful massifs of the continents die away finally to a pitiful end, find their conclusion in a few small stones and the last tiny grains of a sand dune. After a long speech the last word is spoken; in a great symphony, the final note sounds. The rest is silence. Everything dies away and ends—even *Faust,* even Homer's *Odyssey,* even the singing of the birds. This world is only an eon which ends when the stars fall and the trumpets of the last judgment are raised.

First encounter with a delicate problem

In the evening, skin still burning from the sun, an address concerning the spiritual situation of present-day Germany. Since a large number of representatives of leading professions are present, in part very deep-thinking people, a penetrating discussion develops, which I relish, and the other matter of this land—its other historical scene, so to speak—begins to stand out in contrast to the German situation. Above all, it is the racial question which inflames the emotions here and leads to opposing points of view. On the other hand, I am surprised to what degree there also exist overlapping and universal problems which know neither geographical nor chronological boundaries and concern *everyone*. Among these are, for example, the unrest and revolt of the youth, of which educators particularly are well informed. Apparently, only the causes which set off these movements are different. They are determined in each instance by the central problems which exist in a country. Here it is the racial problem: Would not the equality of black and white as a logical result of democratization lead to such a quantitatively enormous preponderance of the African element that the political and historical role the white man has played be over immediately? Hasn't the white man, by reason of his culturally creative accomplishments, legitimized the role of leadership he fulfills? Hasn't each population entity the right to maintain its "racial identity"? Does not every form of integration lead to chaos—as is purportedly seen in the countries of Africa where it has been introduced? For this reason, then, isn't apartheid legitimate?

I have the feeling that the problem broached here as *cantus firmus* will probably determine all South African discussions— just as it did on the earlier trip. It is almost stereotypical how this problem which dominates and separates minds so absolutely comes into discussion immediately and everywhere: what do you think about apartheid? This was true even in the morning when our friends wanted to know whether we also had black students in Hamburg, and then could scarcely conceal their dismay when we told them these students often visited us at our home. But no matter how one decides this question, whether in the conservative direction of radical racial separation or, as the younger people do, for integration—in one respect the disagreeing debators always concur: in their rage against the boundless self-righteousness and priggishness so especially evidenced by the visitors from Germany and by newspaper reporters after their whirlwind visits. When one has wrestled day after day with an absolutely insoluble problem, and when this problem has, besides, a fateful significance for the work of one's forebears and the life of one's descendants, one reacts with the utmost irritability toward the terrible simplificators who, without intellectual and existential expense, propose their primitive and self-assured homemade recipes as *the* solution. One says: "I would just like to know how you in

Germany would behave if you had to deal with this problem. It is easy enough for you to turn your noses up at the racial conflicts in the States or in South Africa."

It is hard for me to take a position here, especially since I would like, first of all, to listen attentively and thus rather play the role of questioner and perhaps also of provocateur. After previous experiences in Africa, I am no longer naïve enough simply to represent a definite position; I still remember very well the disgrace which befell me when I, at that time, cheerfully came out for racial integration on the grounds of humanitarianism and was pinned to the mat with a few expert holds by the then State Secretary for Apartheid Problems. He had thought through the entire complexity of the problem, and I could not answer his critical counterquestions. (He was, by the way, so tactful as to allow my disgrace to exist more in my own moral consciousness than in the form of a public "knockout.")

On one matter, of course, I have a firm and imperturbable point of view, both here and the other morning at the assembly of pastors: I deny that racial separation can be theologically justified. I met with this attempted justification again and again in discussions with Boer theologians. It corresponded to the order of creation, so they were accustomed to arguing, that each was created "after his own kind" and therefore must remain separated from the other kinds. This principle of differentiation also includes the subordination predetermined by the creation of one under the other. Ham, the black man, was now meant for the role of servant. In the face of such argumentation I always became enraged to see the Bible misused for the ideological justification of authority. If that is in itself a blasphemy, it becomes even worse when these people do missionary work. For then their proselytizing smells as if they wanted only to increase the feeling of inferiority in the black people by inoculating them with their Christian ideology, and as if they were using Christianity to stabilize their own rule. For me it was always a sign of the ideological perversion of Christianity, as it is seen in such points of view,

30

when my interlocutor was absolutely incorrigible. Every appeal to dissuade from the nonsense of such fantasies by the study of biblical texts was fruitless. One cannot dispute with ideologues because their thinking does not deal with questions of the truth, but rather with an interest that must be defended, come what may.

It is satisfying for me to see that this time I am forcing a door open with my warning concerning the pseudo-Christian ideologues. Here something has been learned over the past decade, and what was at that earlier time still somewhat widespread is now obviously limited to sectarians on the fringes. It is happy progress—also in regard to Christian ethic—that the apartheid question has been dethologized, that it is now understood purely pragmatically as a sociopolitical problem. Thus one is at least freed from fanaticisms and absolutisms and is open to middle courses for compromises and a certain maneuvering. What else is needed?

Of the very lively theological discussion the other morning, one phase in particular remains in my memory. Naturally I was asked—as I very often am on this journey—about the right of the Ecumenical Council to support revolutionary freedom movements in East African Tanzania. When I expressed my rejection of this resolution and was met, in addition, with widespread agreement, a young lady vicar who worked among mulattos arose and stopped the flood of theoretical arguments. She was moved by the injustice the Africans suffer: the forcible separation of families, the material disadvantage, the political underprivilege. Examples of these things which she experienced daily in her work seemed to gush forth from her. The others made a face because they were obviously acquainted with these plaints. Upon me, however, they did not fail to make an impression. When a person devotes his work and life to something, his words gain credibility and weight, so it made me thoughtful when she spoke not to excuse the brutality and the delusion of those freedom fighters, but rather to change our manner of seeing and the direction of

31

our questions. Should we not, instead of always speaking of the guilt, terror, and cruelty of the freedom fighters, rather first discuss the guilt of those who have brought them to such a point and have thus incited their acts of desperation?

She was, in fact, addressing here a theological problem of great moment: Christian love means not only binding up wounds and being the good Samaritan after the event; it also has the duty of preventing wounds and thereby being effective in a deterrent way. Therefore, it will never merely accuse when confronted with misdeeds but will make effort to stop the source of the misdeeds. This means, however—and this position I also supported in our discussion—that Christian love has a political dimension: it must also consider the social and economic structures in which one can live in peace and not be stimulated to hate, revenge, and disorder. In this sense I tried to extend the New Testament parable of the merciful Samaritan: when the Samaritan arrived at home, he set about to insure that the forests were systematically combed for rapacious elements, so that no one else would fall under the hand of the murderers. Yet more: when finally some dark highwayman had been caught, he saw that his Samaritan love also had an obligation to *this* fellow. As he sought to learn from him why he had become a criminal and perhaps found out in what way he had been suffering from environmental deprivation and childhood trauma (to express it in a somewhat pointedly modern manner), then he could also seek to become involved there and to help out.

I have gotten a little ahead of myself. In the late evening after the address, Pastor D. drove us through the dark streets of "District Six," that slum area where over 60,000 blacks of all shades of skin are crammed into ramshackle houses and huts. One can also imagine the life there by day—the swarms of children, the scurrying and pressing on the narrow streets in front of and in the shops, and on the buses. Even now numerous lost and ragged-looking forms are squatting by walls, doors, and in niches. In the stillness of the night all this has the effect of an abandoned backdrop for a social shockfilm. And yet from this district countless blacks have gone forth to accomplishment and fame as writers on concert podiums, opera stages, and in many other areas.

The day closes with a last drive up to the ridge of the Lion's Head. From there an ocean of countless lights spreads out before us like a sparkling carpet.

Journey to Stellenbosch

On the next morning, which was yesterday, Mr. v. B., as representative of the company, met us for a drive to Stellenbosch. One notices in him the freshness of the young Marine officer and the culture of an old family. And because his South African school and university experiences lie such a short while behind him one can learn something from him about the mentality and direction of development of today's youth.

As we drive from Capetown over National Highway 9 through the gigantic vineyard districts and finally head for the old Huguenot city of Paarl, v. B. makes the first allusions. As a pupil in boarding schools here and later as a student of Stellenbosch University, he knows this small city very well. Faithful to strict Huguenot traditions, one attends church here three times on Sundays. That is obligatory for the many boarding school students. In the meantime, all sports or any other type of playful activity in public is forbidden.

"Then one can only read and crochet?" I ask.

"Crocheting and knitting are certainly permitted," he says, "especially when they are done for charitable causes. But reading is another matter. In the boarding schools, only the Bible and church pamphlets are permitted."

When I cannot suppress a small sound of dismay and consider what anti-effects are produced in this way, v. B. says: "Worse than the quantitative overfeeding, however, is the subject matter of the sermons." This has scarcely anything to do with the gospel, he says, and is in many instances the most rigorous and completely humorless moralism. Thus v. B. himself has heard how the drought of the last years was proclaimed from the pulpit as divine retribution for the fashion of the miniskirt. "When I follow the further path of my fellow students," he says, "I find the same thing again and again. As soon as the pressure is relieved after graduation the religious dictates from school and college are shaken off and the way leads then to nihilism and libertinism. For what one has learned there as Christianity has not only lost every charm but can, in fact, be of absolutely no support in life."

What really got on one's nerves was the widespread hypocrisy. "Of course, under our desks we read *Stern* and *Playboy*. But for the outside world, we played the innocent schoolboy." It was his opinion that among the Stellenbosch students who, like the older ones, were subject to the same pressure, a huge explosion was coming. "Only those who have not followed the results of the psychical seismographs will be surprised." As for v. B., he would not like to give the impression of being emotionally progressive. He is critical enough to see in certain trends of our time not only improvement and change for the better. There is certainly good sense in not simply storming blindly and uncritically forward. "Brakes can certainly be applied to a movement," he considers on the other hand, "but one cannot halt it forcefully. Perhaps South Africa will indeed succeed in attaining a delaying effect of, let's say, twenty years in questions of morality and mentality. But if one tries to go back thirty years, then the screw has been turned one too many times and what it was supposed to hold together can tear apart with a crack." Here is someone who has perceived the subsurface ill-feeling which, to be sure, is noticeable in South Africa not only in this realm.

The drive through the campus of Stellenbosch awakens lively

memories in me of the time when I gave a guest lecture here. The greeting then was unforgettable for me: the young men stood and sang a psalm that thundered in my ears. But what v. B. has just told us has even tarnished the precious image of this place I had held until now.

One notices the dominance of tradition even in the architecture. In spite of the rapidly growing numbers of students here, no skyscrapers have been erected. This is undoubtedly a unique feature! Tradition is held to as a matter of logic. In this land the cultivation of historical memories plays a large role everywhere, and certainly Stellenbosch and Paarl are outstanding examples of that fact. In the farm of Groot Constantia, which we visited near Capetown on Sunday, or in the beautiful Cape-Dutch Town House in Paarl, one is transported in a very real way into the milieu of pioneer days: in a bedroom with a bed surrounded by hangings and the touching cradle which can be tended from the bed; in the comfortable rooms with cabinets, chests, and furniture of noble simplicity. What a liberality of life-style these express! But we also visited the gruesome cellar in which the slaves who made possible the free life in the "Bel Étage" were quartered. Does one column by Phidias, as Treitschke once dared to assert, outweigh all the misery of the slave masses of antiquity? What a culture of hospitality I found on the farms of the southwest! But all that has its price too— Of course, one must avoid thinking unhistorically and measuring each and every thing with the yardstick of one's own time and one's own culture. But it would be just as incorrect if one, on the other hand, went astray and relatively and uncritically measured each time in its own right. One must decide within oneself the conflict of thoughts and feelings which arise in such situations. There is no simple solution.

Once again we meet with history as we lunch in Rawdon's Hotel Lanzerac in Stellenbosch. The company has also invited the church president of the district and his wife, both of whom relish the abundance of delicacies as blissfully as do the missionaries at the Buddenbrook House. But neither are we fastidious. We must even agree that the word "eat" would mean a trivialization here; in the presence of this menu, of the cold buffet and the dessert tables, the only proper word is *feast*. The hall in which we are indulging in this celebration resembles the refectory of an old English university. The memories of the historical background are carefully preserved in other ways too. The rooms of this old, nobly planned farm, which has been converted into a truly "special" hotel, are preserved as much as possible. Among the comfortable waiting rooms, I am particularly impressed by a library study with fireplace, old fire irons, and comfortable lamps. Restaurants of this type which master the charisma of private intimacy I have found in a comparable manner only in Scotland. The stalls of the farm have been changed into guest rooms and surround a beautiful open courtyard. Trees, flowers, and lawns give, in addition, the illusion that one is attending a country party at the house of good friends.

When we return to the ship new passengers have come aboard: Mrs. F. from Johannesburg, whose sense of humor one can perceive even from a distance; Mr. S., a young man from Hamburg who has spent many years in West and South Africa in the service of the ship line, and who is now finally returning to Europe; and Mrs. Sch. from Windhuk, who is greeted by steward and crew with a loud hello. For many years she has been voyaging between Capetown and Beira for pleasure. Everyone knows her and she knows everyone. Nothing human and nothing maritime is strange to her. She knows all the ship-and-shore gossip and, as a delightful old lady, she can tell it charmingly and wittily. At the same time she is a sharp and intelligent observer. Thus there are also many serious conversations with her to which I owe not a little knowledge about the country, the people, and the problems.

In Port Elizabeth

Lumbago and toothache. These evils always seem to come at the most awkward moments. Even when one tries to ignore them, they considerably lessen one's pleasures of perception. Especially the painful grimaces occasioned by lumbago mirror themselves in the facial expressions of others in something of a mixture of sympathy and amusement.

When I think back on the days in Port Elizabeth I scarcely have the feeling of having set foot on African soil. This third largest harbor city of South Africa has, like Capetown, a thoroughly European style and, having so quickly become accustomed to the inversion of the seasons, we easily imagine ourselves transported to an early summer shore on the Mediterranean Sea. Fine beaches, fine parks, generously planned residential suburbs with an emphatically individualistic style—all this is captivating but it is not the Africa of the popular imagination. The skin shades, mainly tending to dark, but rich in many nuances, supply only a faint corrective to this impression. The peculiar situation in South Africa makes itself noticed of course in the fact that all benches, public conveniences, and museum ticket offices display placards which state precisely where are the waiting rooms, rest rooms, and entrances for whites and where those for the people of other skin colors. When we visit the complex of the snake farm, the aquarium, and the dolphin tanks, it strikes me as somewhat ridiculous that here also are adjacent box office entrances, separated according to race, while inside everyone stands and sits together.

Since Mrs. F. keeps a house in great style in Johannesburg and obviously very much enjoys her role as mistress over many black servants (I am convinced that she is a very nice lady, but thoroughly a "lady") I absolutely had to mention my reaction to the black-white ticket windows, and I did it with provocatory ridicule.

She looked at me with exceeding sympathy because I had not seen through the situation. "Didn't you notice the price difference between the entrance fee the whites and the blacks must pay?" she asked. "From the outside it looks as if such separated entrances were only the expression of white snobbery. In reality this is a matter of social motive. The Bantus and the blacks receive a 50 percent discount."

"—And why?" I inquire somewhat sanctimoniously.

"Indeed, they earn much less," she says. "Therefore the whites are made to pay more."

I did not doubt her honest conviction that a social motive was at work here. However, she was perplexed when I countered: "And why do they earn less?" (I note this small conversational intermezzo because it shows how even simple everyday occurrences repeatedly lead back to the basic question of apartheid.)

The social expenditures for the black population in South Africa are indeed considerable. Schools, universities, and welfare institutions of every sort are put at their disposal. They are —and on this question I must believe the unanimous reports of the South Africans—materially better off here than in any other African state. And yet all this takes place upon a level of decided political and economic underprivilege in comparison with the white population—as was symbolized by the ticket office at the herpetarium. But how is one to change this level without bringing down the total structure of life of this state? That is the puzzler no one can answer. And because I myself do not have the answer at my disposal, the gentle mocking with which I involve Mrs. F. in a question-answer game rests upon very weak footing indeed.

In the evening I cannot seem to get in the mood for conversation and am for the most part dull and monosyllabic. Reading the air-mail edition of *Welt* has plunged me into a depression. A Protestant youth group in Hamburg has organized a "Dance of the Dead" with a "Funeral Repast" in mockery of Memorial Day. Such perversities have a particularly depressing effect here far from home where one has no correctives at his disposal to put aright this macabre impression. Certainly not the sight of healthy, unconfused and well-bred youth. Thus one is overcome by such melancholy as is produced by sights of decay and "the decline of the West." But from my many experiences with radical young people I know they would contradict me violently. They want, so they would assert, by no means to mock death and resurrection; they intend rather to "unmask" the bourgeois quality of this custom which has become a cheap cliché. By the same token, the young Hamburg vicars did not wish to ridicule the sacrament when they protested with transparencies the "gobbling" of the sacramental wafer and the "lapping up" of wine. On the contrary, they wanted thematically to make a statement that they were attacking the liturgical ceremonial because it had become a petrified routine. I would like to be fair and not disregard their background motivation. And yet I cannot get away from the impression that the relationship to the sacred substance must be very deeply and perhaps irreparably injured when one blasphemously plays so fast and loose with their form and not even the slightest traces of reverence or piety are evident. Of course, here rages a wrath against bourgeois misrepresentations and abandoned, misused holiness. Does one really want to free this holiness from its infirmity—or is this only the disorderliness of those who can no more see what life is for?

This evening I feel myself surrounded by questions, German and African, for which I see no solution. Reading the Book of Job will do me good. He also felt himself surrounded.

Racial separation: hateful apartheid

Yesterday evening, before we left Port Elizabeth, we had on board some visitors from the city who obviously wanted to enjoy the atmosphere of a German ship and to experience certain luxuries which are to be had more inexpensively here than on land. I soon got into a lively discussion with a young doctor and an intellectually vital, thoughtful, and politically engaged lawyer—naturally, again, about apartheid. I consciously started it myself with a somewhat aggressive remark about the separate black-white entrance gates.

"You may think what you wish about that," the doctor reprimanded me, "but you must admit one thing: in a country with such racial pluralism, each element of the population must have the right to protect its identity!" There again was the slogan with which I had become familiar in Capetown.

"Naturally I must grant you this right. I am only asking myself whether it should occur as it does in South Africa. I simply cannot escape the impression that this petty bureaucratic separation of the races must be thoroughly vilifying for the blacks—disregarding completely for the moment the other disadvantages."

"No one has yet been able to demonstrate to me," the lawyer now interpolated, "what other effective solution there should be. Just look around in Africa, and when you come to the East Coast you will see there with your own eyes, at least, the results of it: where the racial barriers have fallen and the rule of the whites has ended, chaos and bloodbaths in the name of Uhuru and emancipation have become the order of the day. The horrors of the Mau Mau and the mass exterminations in the Congo are only a couple of examples. It is not only the whites who have suffered. Everywhere the whites are driven out the economy declines. You will undoubtedly be able to observe the disorganization on this trip. And, if you please, what do you see around you here? A flourishing economy, order, and no massacres. That is saying much for present-day Africa, and it is an absolute exception. Besides, a great deal is being done for the nonwhites, completely aside from the fact that they have their full measure in the growing prosperity. You are aware of that, too. Why else would the Africans come here in thousands from the neighboring countries to work and earn? Do you think that would be the case if we beat our blacks every day or threw them to the crocodiles? The ideas of us that people on the outside have seem to tend in this direction. We are just not good enough to be permitted to take part in international sporting competitions, much less in the Olympics!"

The last words sounded quite bitter. I thought of the nice young representative of our company who was a top athlete of his country and who—although no word was said about it—certainly suffered from the fact that the racial politics of his country precluded any competition with foreign comrades. But was it really the general principles of apartheid against which the outside world reacted with a boycott of South African athletes? Wasn't the boycott, above all, set off precisely because only *whites* could represent South Africa athletically, and was it not this with which the outside world could not reconcile itself?

However, I wish to remain with the real theme and not to divert our conversation to a sidetrack. In order to encourage my new acquaintances to express themselves in an uninhibited manner, and to prevent this highly explosive issue from being discharged in emotions, I wanted first to dispel the evident suspicion that I was one of those know-it-alls who likes to attack with cheap criticism and cheap advice from the secure fortress of his principles. I told them candidly that in my first South African trip I had not lost my impulse for critical inquiries but had, on the other hand, forfeited all pharisaical attitudes toward their country. I said I was no longer as naive as the average newspaper reader on the outside. And to introduce one respect where they would find no prejudice and reservations in me, I said to them: "It is completely clear to me that the presence of whites in South Africa is not founded upon a theft of land from the legitimate inhabitants, the Africans. I know that when the Dutch-East Indies Company settled there, no one lived in the Cape country outside of a few Hottentots and Bushmen and that the Bantus poured in only later or approximately at the same time. As regards the legitimacy of colonization, you need have no fear of polemics from me. Neither will I belabor you with that abusive term *colonialism*. Finally, in view of the fact the Boers have been the vanguard against European colonialism, I find it silly when those who fought against the colonial ambitions of Great Britain are denounced as "colonial masters."

In order to avoid setting up a false front in our conversation, I added to the last opinion: "I am also quite aware that the coexistence of very different races with just as different stages of development presents inherent problems, about which any judgment from the outside—above all, in the name of a pale equalitarian humanitarian ideology—must bear the verdict of being highly foolish. And because I am so uncertain and am confronted by so many open questions, I am extremely curious to hear from you what you see as the purpose of your racial politics. The mere stabilization of racial difference can certainly not be an end in itself."

My dialogue partners, I believe, were not hardened partisans. Otherwise I could have inferred their answers from correspondingly programmed explanations. I had the feeling that they possessed a healthy common sense and an open mind. Therefore, I hoped to hear convictions rooted in their own thoughts.

"I consider it good that you are asking about the purpose of our racial politics," said the doctor. "For that gives us opportunity to refer you to the fact that the present status of apartheid is, in fact, only an interim, a period of transition within a development planned on a long-term basis."

"Does that mean," I immediately broke in, "that you have in view an end to racial pluralism, a miscegenation, perhaps, an integration—in any case, beginning at a certain date?"

"Certainly not that! I have already spoken of the maintenance of racial identity. Rather it is a matter of increasing the spatial separation of racially different populations, of marking out proper territories, and of the relative autonomy of component nationalities which have been consolidated."

"Just a moment," I interjected, "what does 'relative autonomy' mean here? Does that mean that the various races and, accordingly, the various tribal areas in which they are to live as their homelands, will be represented equally and with the appropriate vote in the Central Parliament of the Republic?"

"Heavens, no!" he cried with horrified face and uplifted hands. "We are, of course, only thinking of a limited, supervised autonomy. Can't you imagine what would happen to us with a proportional vote of the African population! Then we would certainly come immediately under the blades of the sled—to express myself in a manner somewhat strange to the African climate."

"I believe that's exactly where the rub is," I agreed. "The overwhelming majority of blacks seems to me to be the really essential problem. The whites feel themselves not only the 'qualified minority' and thus the historically justified governing class, but they feel themselves, above all, to be the *quantitative* minority who are bucking the democratic trend of our time. A democracy, the function of which is based upon the equality of all, and the decisions of which are made by proportional vote, would be fatal for the white minority. Ergo: since this minority feels itself qualified for the role of government, it must deny the democratic principle of quantity. It *cannot*, therefore, ever want something like the political equality of all races. Thus I ask myself whether many extreme forms of apartheid so annoying to the visitor are not founded upon this *fear*—upon the fear that one could be overwhelmed in the long run by the numerical superiority of the blacks and their explosive rate of propagation. One need only see the teeming hordes of Negro children everywhere to understand this fear. It could also be true here that, with a certain increase, quantity could change to quality and new circumstances of rule could be brought about by way of revolution. In saying this, I disregard completely the possibility of Communist infiltrations or that the Africans' will to freedom could be ideologically stirred up from the outside. My instincts have deceived me in a most improbable manner if I haven't observed this expression of fear again and again. It is to be read in faces, and it often conceals itself in subordinate clauses. . . . Please excuse my long speech, but these questions have really gotten under my skin."

One of the ladies who had been listening with lively interest commented that it was precisely because of this "fear" that it was so difficult to discuss apartheid. No one who lives here, she said, was impartial in regard to this question. However, where fear ruled, she continued, people are just as immune to arguments as when the wish is father to the thought.

The lawyer, objecting somewhat, said there was no possibility for understanding at all; one could no longer hope to reach a measure of objectivity through all the emotions and involvement. After all, he said, there was something called intellectual discipline, and his profession had given him some instruction in this. Then he turned to me: he did not wish, he said, to feign an exaggerated self-confidence nor to behave as if what I had said about fear was totally groundless. "We do not, in fact, know what the future brings. And when we try to compute the development of the quantities with the slide rule, things look rather bad. For myself, I answer all the matters we have discussed here with one conviction, which can be illustrated from the history of our country and which gives me hope. I mean the superiority of the white race. This will remain as evident as always and will continually find new ways to assert itself."

My skepticism toward apartheid; but good advice is expensive

"Are you really so certain about that?" I asked. "Here I must express my skepticism. In the U.S.A. I spoke with not a few intellectual blacks, mostly at universities, about this question. Quite aside from the fact that my interlocutors betrayed no symptoms of inferiority, I was impressed above all by their argument that the inferiority of the black population did not reside in a biological-racial negative, but in social discrimination, lack of education, poor training, as well as in underprivileges of every sort. In the racial phariseeism of the whites is thus seen, perhaps, an extreme self-delusion, if not an illusion with a purpose, by which is sought to camouflage an historical guilt in regard to the black man. I have just been reading Anne Moody's book *Growing Up on the Mississippi* and I must say that it has greatly strengthened me in my suppositions. When I consider what that could mean for South Africa, then a brief remark and question will suffice. You, Mr. B., have erected good schools and even universities for the nonwhites and thus aim at a class of corresponding intelligence. Do you consider it possible to maintain this group in the status of second-class citizenship and to preserve the hierarchical structure of the races? Would not all that be undermined by the principle of achievement and competition? You certainly cannot provide an equal education—and, happily, that is what you intend!—and then grant to those thus educated inferior rights and lesser remuneration in professional life! In an open job competition, would it not necessarily come to black bosses and white subordinates—simply because the achievement levels so correspond in individual cases? Then, however, to discriminate against the blacks in their rights and wages would lead to quite grotesque distortions—not to mention the psychological tinder which accumulates in this manner. The violence of the explosion to come can be imagined to some degree."

My acquaintances did not really take up this vision of the future, which was meant as a question. Perhaps I had expressed a thought which lay much too near to them, one which they had turned over in their minds hundreds of times already without having found a solution. The doctor would only say evasively that things were really much more complicated than that. Of course, there could be special cases of unusual aptitude among the Bantus, he said, although he had observed something like that only in certain professions.

"Also in your own profession?" I asked.

"Of course," he replied. "There are a number of outstanding doctors, especially surgeons, but hardly any architects and engineers. But these outstanding aptitudes do not form the essential problem. If one observes the entire situation, then one must know without doubt that there is no such thing as *the* black man. The people with black skin consist of a great number of tribes, quite variously endowed and existing upon quite different levels of culture. Of some I would truly say that they are really not educable. No training, no matter how carefully planned, will lift them above a very limited level."

I must have looked somewhat skeptical when these words were spoken (not because I could give counterarguments, but because I am allergic to all biological prejudices in the human area, which I admit does not exactly increase my impartiality!). In any case, my partners in the dialogue were now ready with many examples which were supposed to demonstrate to me the limits in the black man of the powers of apprehension, initiative, responsible self-sufficiency, and many other virtues of humanity. Even Albert Schweitzer was quoted in some of his highly critical judgments about the blacks. "And he really tried everything! His doctrine of the sanctity of all life, which extended even to animals, prevented him, of course, from establishing a monopoly of rulership by the white man with a corresponding deprecation of the Africans. Finally, it was bitter *experiences* which led him against his ideas of humanity to his discovery that one cannot depend upon the black people; when they do not feel the lash of the white master, they sit on their backsides and let everything go to waste."

Of course, that was not very convincing, but it made a certain impression on me nevertheless. What the doctor said especially haunts my memory, for he was fair enough to report also of the more favorable sides of the blacks, and I received from what he said the impression of sober-minded thoughtfulness.

Now a younger man, who had been silent up to this time but who had been listening very attentively, joined in the conversation. I gathered, from references he made later, that he was employed in an academic capacity. Turning to the lawyer and the doctor, he took up again what had been said at the beginning of the conversation concerning the ultimate goal of the government. "You said that apartheid must be transformed into a more geopolitical concept. There is supposed to be eventually a multitude of relatively autonomous homelands for the nonwhite population. Excuse me, but I consider this a gigantic illusion! I will give only two reasons, the first, a historical one. We are a pluralistic society in South Africa, resembling a racial scrambled egg, a mixture of the most various ingredients, which came into being several centuries ago. It is no longer possible to dissolve this conglomerate by means of chemical-political reagents. The second point I would like to bring up against the idea of racial territories is derived from a simple economic consideration. In spite of all apartheid and in spite of all the differences of rights, the races have long ago been integrated into the economic process. This development will continue and in any case is irreversible. Industrial production, as well as services, has operated as a melting pot. If it ever came to the point—to give an extreme example—that the racial groups were isolated in their own territories, it would lead to a total crippling of the economy. What would the whites do if they wanted to live alone without the black workers? And without the black servants in their houses and hotels? And how would the territories of the Africans develop if the racial theory of their deficient self-sufficiency is correct—or even if it is *not* correct and a destructive competition arises among them? When, however, the whites build their factories on the black reservations in order to escape these various dangers, a governing white class must also be there. And so the screws would begin to turn all over again."

I have the feeling that a point has been reached at which the hopelessness of the problem is seen in all its oppressive but nevertheless desirable clarity. By "hopelessness" I mean that there is no solution which would be clearly satisfactory for both sides and without all-too-explosive stimulation for new conflicts. Here no distant utopian goals offer themselves. Here one can only muddle along, maneuver, and see how one gets through the constantly changing play of forces. Not only does the game change, but also the opponents.

Meanwhile it has become too late to continue the discussion. The steward announces that the ship is preparing to cast off, and only a few friends are exchanging their farewells in the salon when I finally say to the circle of debaters: "It has once again become clear to me how naive are all those people who sit outside Africa on their high horses and bray insipid slogans about what one really should do. One becomes more modest as a visitor in this country if he keeps his eyes open and considers a little—which does not preclude that he remain critical and not conceal his displeasure about this or that. And in the practice of apartheid there is much I do not understand."

Farewells are exchanged. When will we see one another again, if at all? Good-bys in exotic harbors are more definite and final than in train stations at home.

In East London

"Quite an intimate harbor, isn't it?" says the captain when we are tied up and have taken a leisurely look around. "Not large, rounded with green hills, and the anticipated pleasure of fine beaches—what more could one want?" He does not seem to be very enthusiastic about the harbor operation itself, although in comparison to what we are to experience in East Africa, ideal circumstances prevail here. "Our stay here will be rather long," he says, "and the reason for that is very characteristic: the crane and fork-lift operators must be whites. However, there are not enough of them. So we must wait." This strikes me as quite mad. En route we saw Africans using the heavy excavation shovels in road construction. That, then, was entrusted to them. And outside those areas dominated by apartheid, of course, they operate all the loading and unloading machines. When the principle of apartheid becomes an article of belief it obviously makes necessary the constant creation of symbolic gradations, as here a certain hierarchy in the use of the machines. When we speak about this at dinner, Mr. S. relates a circumstance I can scarcely believe and also cannot verify. Nevertheless he assures me that it is true, and, after all, he is an authority of many years standing: In Capetown some years ago there was a serious shortage of white fork-lift operators, so that blacks had to be used. In order to emphasize the distance between black and white, a special construction was installed so that the operator sat not upon the saddle but had to walk alongside the machine.

We expected nothing special from East London as a city, except, of course, the beautiful beaches. But that we were not supposed to get our hopes up had already been made clear to us when we saw the "Main Post Office" emphasized in the guidebook as a tourist attraction. Our drive through the city revealed

49

the same comfortless wasteland of small-town planlessness and that lack of character which one often finds in provincial cities in America. Coca Cola signs, filling stations, and supermarkets press in upon the memory when one thinks back and asks himself what he has really seen. The suburbs, on the other hand, are impressive. Here again I am struck by their individualism. No house is like any other, and the difference by no means consists in variations of one style. At the same time, there is not the impression here of a chaotic jumble. That which has aesthetic quality—and one cannot deny that in this architecture—in the final estimation fits in, and the blooming gardens form transitions to soften all too crass contrasts. We northern people, having just come from a stern late autumn, always get the feeling of being literally attacked by the flashing colors of the flamboyant bright scarlet trees, the blue jacarandas, and the bewildering variegations of the garden flowers.

But even here the elements lurk behind the peace of this comfort and ease. The traces of last year's flood catastrophe are still recognizable everywhere. Even the high bridge we cross, so the driver tells us, was formerly under water, and the villa on the shore, its erstwhile splendor still suggested by the ruins, was shattered by the raging flood.

It is enjoyable to have with us Mrs. F. from Johannesburg, a cheerful, older lady who likes to be teased and who gladly takes part in the escapades of foolishness which sometimes come over us in the exuberance of our travel moods. When once I mentioned her "happy nature" to her, she said: "I was brought up to see the positive in everything, so I am always content." This condition is not to be taken for granted, although she is well situated and, measured by European standards, has access to a fabulous number of servants. Several times in this country we have already met bored women who suffer from the emptiness of a life in which every duty has been taken away from them. Contentment of the sort which emanates from Mrs. F. is probably either a happy gift of the internal constitution or a creative act of mind over matter. Such a person does uncommon good to a skeptical disposition like mine, especially in the untroubled atmosphere of a ship.

But just as I was sitting in the deck chair this afternoon meditating upon such things, I was oppressed by a thought which came to me in reading Anne Moody's life story about the blacks' thorny struggle for freedom in America. She tells how once she fell into a great rage when she saw laughing, contented blacks on the street. For her all these people are "Uncle Toms," a term of reproach she and her friends use for members of their race who are content with their fate, are adjusted, and now indulge in laissez-faire with good humor and ease. If Mrs. F. were black, if she did not belong to the ruling class in South Africa, her contentment and her "happy nature" would also suffer the scorn of Anne Moody. But even as things are, she would undoubtedly reproach Mrs. F. with the fact that one cannot wage racial or class struggles with her type, and that her contentment is only the comfortable disposition of her privileged caste.

Who is right? The question disturbs me. Contentment, optimism, and cheerfulness—the Roman speaks of *serenitas* and *hilaritas*—are, if I judge without bias, beautiful human attributes. If I do not succeed, especially as a Christian, in attaining them, then I reproach myself. Then I have the feeling that I have not realized the potential of my humanity. The person who is on bad terms with God, the world, and his fellow-man, and who lives in constant negation, is to me abysmally pitiable. Is it not dreadful and the beginning of ideological narrow-mindedness when one measures all human qualities only by the objective of a specific activity, by function? When one can no more use the fullness of human nature because it does not produce enough fanaticism for class or racial struggle? When one can use only thus those deficient beings who are directed at one goal? Must one not also damn humor then because it surmounts the world with a smile and therefore invalidates fanatical attitudes? Even here I have already seen white and black faces fixed in determination, upon which

51

no yes of any sort is written. Were we not struck also by the lack of humor and self-irony in the fanatics of the student rebellion?

If the young people were asked about this (such conversations did occur now and then) they answered that humor and self-irony robbed them of the fuel for their actions. They needed fanaticism to gain conviction for their madness. Their only kind of laughter was the laughter of scorn. But I question whether that is not weakness, whether the real human sovereignty could not consist in the power of affirming that which is beautiful in life, of finding in one's enemy that which is worthy of affirmation, of being able to appreciate the ethos of opposing attitudes—and simultaneously of taking a firm stand, not glossing over differences, and yet persisting in the fight. In his *Marlborough*, Churchill depicts qualities in his forebears which show this tendency. People engaged in dreadful battles, but then bowed to others. As the conclusion to the negation of the day's battle, there was a final affirmation.

East London
Eternity Sunday, November 22

Today we were at the service in the German Andreas Church together with Mr. S. and were harshly disappointed. Instead of a pastor two lay readers conducted the service and read the liturgy and sermon. Were they of such unusually simple natures that they always misread and mumbled unintelligibly besides? Or had they not read their texts in advance? Everything else was also as impersonal as possible. No one spoke to us, and when I took the initiative to speak, I was answered in a somewhat surprised and faintly rejecting manner. Was it like this in the other churches too, out of which poured broad streams of people? In America it was always such a good feeling to be immediately welcomed into the congregation.

How seldom one takes part in a church service which goes to

one's marrow and causes him to experience the spiritual power of God's Word in a living congregation. *When* it does happen, it gives the most uplifting joy one can encounter. In fact, I still draw sustenance from the few times I have experienced it.

In the afternoon when we returned from swimming, feeling wonderfully refreshed, the steward slipped the newly popular pornographic magazine *Jasmin* into my hand. His somewhat skeptical smile indicated a certain doubt concerning my receptivity. He guessed rightly. When one has moved some weeks in the realm of the elements and has enjoyed the therapeutic effects of distance, these portraits of the financial ostentation of the jet set or of the nihilism of a ruined aristocracy are especially depressing. These are the images which are poured into the soul by mercantile interests! The inane instruction given to the erotically untalented, a special class for which each detail must be premasticated countless times; the lecturing of "psychologists" without criteria, who want to be progressive without regard to losses—oh, that disgusts me to the highest degree for *moral* reasons, as in my mind I see the many scavengers in the background, those vultures of capitalism for whom any filth is good enough to turn to account! (The so-called ultraleftists of the young generation who are usually on a constant hunt for capitalistic motives, ride happily along on the commercially produced sex wave and seem to have a blind spot in respect to this.)

In general, I am sorry about the consumption of sex.

What will happen to a younger generation which becomes acquainted with such distorted sexuality and does not see through the bogus pedagoguery and moral iconoclasm? What the Creator intended for the joy and fulfillment of life here becomes the material of boredom and the emptiness of perpetual sameness. The pornographic St. Pauli newspapers are at least honest and display their commercial lasciviousness openly. This virtue is, of course, highly relative and exists only in comparison with the graphically virtuoso emptiness of *Jasmin*. Total hollowness in the poor ones who stand in the shadows is not noticeable.

Nouveau riche hollowness, however, which puffs itself up and preens itself, and, at the same time, flourishes in the accumulation of tastelessness, has a much more penetrating effect. And it is this element in the magazine which nauseates me.

Before Durban
November 23

At anchor in the vicinity of Durban. We lie in the middle of a gigantic chain of hills covered by dwellings which are camped before the modern complex of skyscrapers. They remind me of New York—in the opposing light forming an imposing panorama which seems to slip away. Five ships lie about us rocking patiently. Although this waiting time—it is to last until tomorrow morning—will somewhat throw us off schedule we are not sad. We are like an island in an ocean of sunlight. One can make waiting an art, producing anticipation and making the arrival of the moment desirable. In any case, this is so when one is looking forward to fun. And we are indeed. That is also the secret of Advent, the new season which is approaching in all its power. The Bible texts of this week are full of promises.

The voyage to our anchorage took us along the African coast. Through our binoculars we observed long stretches of pathless, uninhabited, virgin lands. The closer we got to Durban the more it was dotted with cities, spas, enchanting country homes, and industrial areas. The fresh wind keeps the heat from being oppressive so that everyone on board plays, chats, takes photographs, dozes in a deck chair or climbs to the poop deck with spyglass and camera.

When the representative of the company in East London who so tirelessly drove us to the swimming pool and all around the area wished us a Merry Christmas, we Europeans were struck with the fantastic situation—that he would be expressing this wish in this most abundant springtime amid summerlike heat!

We will have to gradually learn that everything is reversed here: that the sun does not move clockwise but counterclockwise; that the crescent moon is upside down, and that this time we will celebrate Christmas in summer heat.

In Durban: a stroll through the city

This morning we entered the harbor in a chilly rain and tied up at the pier directly next to the bathing area. Our games leader and cheerleader at shuffleboard, Mr. W. from Hamburg, and Mrs. F. said good-by. Mrs. F. has recently received the news that her favorite cat had kittens and then shortly afterward was run over. So there was a tearful good-by. The fun of her Johannesburg idyll has been overshadowed by this small tragedy. L.* receives a beautiful corsage as a sign of welcome.

In the evening. We have just returned from an excursion to the north, where it rained buckets. It would have been like this at home on a gray November day, only here we don't have to freeze.

From Durban we drove out to the Salt Rocks over "N 14," a brand-new state highway. A variant of earlier colonial splendor, the beach hotel in which we drank tea high above the sea reminds me of Beverly Hills. Barefooted Indian workers labor on the terraces. Indian waiters in great number serve us quietly and quickly. At the next table an ancient Englishwoman with a slightly trembling head sits and drinks her tea with ceremonial dignity and extended fingers. On the way back the strongest im-

---

* "L." signifies in the diary the first name of my wife. According to her wish I limit reference to her to the minimum.

55

pression upon me is of the Indian town Tongaat with its over-flowing mass of people. The colorfulness of the clothing, the glistening necklaces, the window displays—even the crowd in the open shops is bright on this grey rainy day. Neither do the harshly lighted supermarkets represent a cool sprinkle of mercantile rationality, but accompany in the colorful dance. This tropical crowd in a Hamburg mist has a peculiar charm. Our black driver, David, who is at our disposal for the week at Durban, is a dignified, friendly man with an extremely relaxed and sure style of driving.

Durban
November 25

The sun has again driven off the clouds of yesterday and now burns down upon us hotly. We visit the wide hall of the Indian market and shop where the crowds of people press among the endless stands. We are almost the only white people. We are surrounded by an enormous curtain of sound. The people bargain temperamentally and with a sporting display of energy. The air is permeated with spices and human exhalations. It is almost unbearable at the meat stands where the cadavers hanging out in the open in the moist heat are covered with myriads of flies.

In the city and on the beach the Zulu coolies who pull the rickshaws are splendidly decorated: a colorful head ornament a yard high which looks like the Arc de Triomphe, the head with gigantic colorfully painted horns, so that without the brown faces one would think of a manifestation of Wotan. The men are hung from head to foot with colorfully decorated carpet. And this gigantic burden is carried in this heat! In running they make the rickshaws bounce along rhythmically. I could not allow myself to be so transported by a human being. Every other service, no matter how inferior, nevertheless has some humane feature. The uncertainty one has about such services is probably caused less by the difficulty of the work than by its symbolism of human subjugation. It is a vestige of slavery. Besides, these highly decked-out human horses know how attractive they are and allow themselves to be photographed for no small gratuity. If they are paid a bit more than average, then they additionally stage a tribal dance accompanied by howling.

I am struck by the way the streetworkers do their hammering in group rhythm and sing at the same time. We are told that a leader spontaneously composes couplets which are then taken up by the group. The subject of these couplets is usually their boss, and their singsong tells whether he is a good or a bad master, whether he takes care of his people or neglects them, whether he pays them punctually or exploits them. Thus the listening public immediately knows all about him, and I can well imagine it is not a matter of indifference to the boss whether the songs are of praise or criticism.

In the Hluhluwe Game Preserve in Zululand

Durban
First Sunday in Advent, November 29

The lumbago I have sought to ignore up to now has gained revenge for my neglect of it. I am lying somewhat helplessly in my cabin absorbed in my Churchill. Only the Bible reading helps me recognize that today is the First Advent. I meditate upon the texts and think of the solemn services at home. Occasionally, however, I pull myself together and look out to see the heavy granite blocks weighing from eight to twelve tons being lifted from the railroad cars into the hold. The great cranes on the pier cannot handle these burdens, but the hoists of the ship can do it.

When the pain became almost unbearable and made the

diagnosis of lumbago seem doubtful to me, I had a doctor come on board who was very nice and thoughtful. Against my will he prescribed a gigantic amount of painkiller and sleeping pills for me which were delivered in the evening by a courier. I took nothing, however, because it could not be determined by the boxes which medicine was which. On the labels it said only: "Take three times a day," or, "To be taken before retiring." As I then learned, medicines are treated as secret products here, the type and character of which is none of the patient's business. They are taken from the factory boxes and put into anonymous bottles and tins so that only the doctor and the druggist are able to tell by the code number of the label what they are. Our officers, who seek to entertain me upon my "bed of pain," can tell some peculiar things about this. For instance, if one has a sore throat he cannot go to the respective specialist but must first go to a general practitioner, who, after receiving his fee then refers the patient to the specialist. The X-rays which were to be made of my spine—I snapped my fingers at that idea, however!—were only prescribed in order to feed the apparatus. One cannot obtain the good alleviating medicines here which are prescribed for lumbago at home.

But I've gotten a little ahead of myself. In spite of the slowly increasing pain, we left on Thursday to drive for two days with the captain into the Hluhluwe (pronounced Shlooshleevee) Game Preserve. In the brooding, dripping heat, with our faithful driver David at the wheel we reached our Zululand Safari Lodge after a drive of several hours through a wild landscape directly adjacent to the preserve. Finding a modern, air-conditioned hotel in the middle of the wilderness after that kind of journey was almost unbelievable. With such an emancipation from the pressure of the heat and the clouds of dust of the road, our enjoyment of this comfort was not in the least diminished by the accusation that we were indulging in a certain snobbism. The guest apartments are small, round, straw-covered structures grouped around the main building in imitation of a Zulu village. Here, too, we were received with every comfort, from the air-conditioning to the perfect bathrooms and elegant color combinations. For just one moment I had to ask myself if it were not a gigantic kitsch—a parody in pop art—to find the primitive world imitated by the last word in civilized design. In conversation about it, however, we decided not to judge so harshly. Even if a cultural oasis were built here, the customary standard German concrete box would certainly be incomparably more dreadful. From a distance this lodge, in any case, does not appear to be a foreign body in the otherwise untouched landscape, but rather is a part of it and an example of living culture.

After these favorable meditations we began the registration battle. When the receptionist learned we were from Hamburg, she beamed, "Our lodge is full of Germans," intending to give us special pleasure. "In fact, there are ten young ladies here with their manager. Quite beautiful girls." This somewhat puzzling information was later explained when we strolled around the swimming pool. There in obviously the best cheer we saw our good captain swimming about in lively conversation with a variety of twittering femininity. Relaxing easily in floating deck chairs, the girls were being photographed incessantly. They seemed to be accustomed to it, for they persisted in long photogenic poses. When they did move, it was wtih lightning speed to display their charms in a new pose. One could scarcely speak here of the unconsciousness of charm as defined in Kleist's *Marionette Theatre.*

While he was swimming and conversing, the captain had found out what and whom this was all about, and the Durban newspapers confirmed it later. The girls were ten "cover-girl models" a somewhat notorious German illustrated magazine—at least notorious according to my ideas!—had chosen in a contest among its readers. It was somewhat sobering to run across this type of press propaganda here. In areas where one still sees good hand-carved faces among both whites and blacks, these empty doll-visages give a rather bad impression of present-day Germany.

The feeling of unpleasantness grew when we met them again in the dining room; even at the table the girls were dressed in only slightly more than bathing suits. The manager had his shirt tied together in front, under which his fat belly bulged—truly a noble representation of old Germany! I was amused by the black waiters who stood lined up against the wall like a phalanx, their eyes almost popping out of their heads while they obviously were trying to pretend disinterest.

The friends who recommended the less spoiled Hluhluwe Game Preserve instead of the more strongly commercialized and Americanized Krueger Park were certainly right. During the entire day we met only two other cars. Guided by a native, we saw everything the park had to offer: horned impala, gazelles, wild boar, zebras and much other wild game, but especially the white-lipped rhinoceroses, which were soaking their powerful bodies in a marshy stream and allowed us to come rather close to them. All the zebras we saw awaited our approach in calm although rather tense curiosity only to dash away at a gallop at the last moment. Meanwhile, the royal eyes of the giraffe, which seem to be shadowed by long eyelashes, regarded us from over their treetops in silent attention and with unspeakable sadness. When these gigantic animals too finally leaped away from our approach, their movements, extending many yards in height, gave the impression of slow motion.

But the memory of the landscape remains much deeper than the encounters with the animals: the rolling chains of hills which disappear in the distant horizon; one single green moving ocean, not dried out as one would almost expect in the searing heat today, but bursting with full colors and abundant vegetation from the great rainfall of the last weeks. The well-paved and splendidly laid-out road allowed us to enjoy the panoramas fully. It is as if a little of the Black Forest highway had been transported to South Africa. When the eye sweeps over this untouched green area it is possible to imagine this landscape as settled also, and it may be the memory of the Black Forest which caused us to think how easily in that valley would fit a little village with houses clustered around a church. That level, slightly rolling plain over there could have cultivated fields divided up like a chessboard. One could imagine the hill over there crowned by the ruins of a castle and on the horizon the haze of a distant city. . . . But it is not so. All this is untouched wilderness which has existed from the beginning. But Württemberg or the mountain land of my home could once have looked like this.

In the evening, famished at first, but now well fed, we sit for a long time under the star-sprinkled heavens, while tongues loosen and conversation has no end. We share many common interests with the captain. Quite aside from the sea voyage, we have the same pleasure in observing people, and also in our interest in problems which we seek to work out in hand-to-hand discussions. Most importantly, we are on the same wave-length in all areas of humor. And so we hatch the clever scheme of tricking the passengers of our *Tanganyika* with the ten cover-girls. We actually succeed, when we return, in convincing them all that the girls have gladly accepted an invitation from the captain to give a fashion show on board. The carpenter is directed immediately to begin work on the runway. But of course our sly steward sees through the matter immediately. He is no kill-joy, though, and wrings his hands in mock despair over how he will be able to prepare the necessary food. Mr. S. is so obsessed by the prospect of an invasion of feminine beauty that he cancels other appointments and takes an early post on the railing so as not to miss the arrival of this prize-winning display of pulchritude. He obviously has also dressed himself up to make an impression on the ladies. Later we admire the equanimity with which he conceals his disappointment and which allows him to behave as if he had seen through our ruse all along.

The next morning we enjoy the English custom of awakening to a strong and aromatic cup of tea, gracefully served at bedside by a liveried stewardess. When we go outside later, a storm is raging around us, sweeping over the entire vista of the wilderness. We will not be able to make the hoped-for trip to Santa Lucia Bay which was to have taken us past crocodiles and sharks. The lodge has been notified by telephone that the planned excursion is not possible because of the storm. But we are taken there by car so that we can at least see the landscape, the deeply cut bay and the foaming sea lashed by the storm. Everywhere there are signs which warn of crocodiles and sharks, and the horror stories about foolish tourists who are attacked by these outlaws so excite our fantasy that we seem to see them ourselves.

A black university

On the return journey we notice on a mountain near Empangeni imposing building complexes which, from a distance, give the impression of a castle. David informs us, not without pride, that this is the Zulu university. Without further ado, we asked to be driven there, and I am amazed at this magnificent modern establishment. It has nothing of the usual emptiness of purely functional utilitarian structures. The numerous buildings, distributed in fine proportions over the countryside, have very individual accents, but are related to one another by unique architectural style. A stone latticework is both a constantly repeated motif and an effective shield from the sun. Luxuriant vegetation enlivens the architecture everywhere, softening its effect and giving it the rhythm of light, shadow, and color. Many courtyards and gardens here and there provide a flowing variegation and even impart idyllic features to this place of study. The library —the only large structure of concrete—includes storage areas which contain many hundreds of thousands of books. The captain looks in the card catalog for my name and to his pleasure finds a quite nice little packet. The large dormitories, separated according to sexes, have an occupancy of about fifteen hundred students. Anyone who comes from the throng of the German mass universities can only look with envy upon this ratio of space to student population.

Since this is a vacation period and this is the noon break, everything is empty. We meet only a few secretaries who provide us with information materials. The faculty and administration still consist mostly of whites, but there is, as a future goal, a real Zulu university with native teachers. The natural sciences are obviously well fitted out with equipment. At the present there are three faculties, the programs of which are somewhat adventurously mixed and richly eclectic: first, the College of Arts, with language departments (Afrikaans, Dutch, and Bantu dialects as well as English and German), political economy, theological subjects, political science, psychology, and philosophy. The student goal here is the bachelor of arts. Then there is the College of Education with history, philosophy, and the psychology of education, as well as practical methodology and pedagogical administration. Here the doctorate can also be obtained. Finally, there is the College of Science, with botany, chemistry, geography, mathematics, physics, psychology, and zoology. These offerings and the requirements are not yet up to the standard of a European university or the colleges of Pretoria and Stellenbosch. But this Zulu institution of learning, like the others which have been constructed for the natives, is planned for growth and future development. If one seeks to measure the prospects as they are represented in the magnificence of this campus, one begins to take seriously the government's intention of culturally advancing the Bantus. If one does that, however, there is the question which was already asked earlier: how the African who has become intellectually self-sufficient would be able to maintain himself in political, social, and economic second-class citizenship. If this is not a possibility, then how does the regime see its own future?

As we continue in the car I read a pamphlet with the conditions of study and the dormitory rules. I have to smile when I think how even the longest hair of a German student would stand on end when reading that one is not to leave the university campus without permission. There is to be no absence from campus overnight without written permission of the rectorship. The prohibition of alcoholic beverages, indeed even their mere possession, is the one heavily underlined rule in the entire book. No newspaper, no publication, be it a book or an essay, may be passed around without the permission of the rector. And even he can give the permission only after the previous agreement of the senate. The young ladies may not leave their dormitory after 7:00 P.M., except with the permission of the housemother. And, of course, the rooms of the girls are absolutely taboo for the male students. It would be next to impossible to persuade the housemothers to make an exception here! But one must not see these strict regulations as merely representative of the white-black, master-boy relationship. Rather a certain understanding of the speed with which the steps between bush primitivity and the *bel étage* of academia have been so quickly by-passed is necessary. Certainly there are a great many academic and pedagogical problems here of which we culturally homogenized Europeans can have no conception. That the situation could easily be strained, that something could get out of joint and therefore need especial disciplinary supports, is not to be overlooked by a perceptive observer.

Durban
November 30

Yesterday, with Mr. K. and his young wife in their small but pretty apartment high above the sea. Mr. K. is the son of a captain with whom I voyaged earlier, and he takes great pains in helping us to organize our stay on land. On the way to their apartment, we attend a competition of Zulu tribal dancers who make their appearances on stage in wildly costumed groups with fearful shouts and piercingly whistled signals. For me, however, the enjoyment is past when I notice the show-business attitude toward the tourists. What one gets to see here of strained and forcefully conserved primitivity is just as boring and insipid as the archaic folk dances and costumed groups in upper Bavaria during the tourist season. We quickly leave this artificial masquerade.

Today peaceful reading with miserable weather. It rains again and again and is extremely humid. In the afternoon we want to stretch our legs a little, and we stroll to a large English passenger ship en route from Australia to London which is tied up at a nearby pier. This gleaming white giant, with its brightly sparkling chains of lights, in the evening looks from a distance like a floating fairy tale and thus awakens our interest and curiosity. If we first feel ourselves the lower class from a freight ship on a visit to a palace and have to struggle with our timidity, our self-confidence is again quickly regained, however. With their plastic chairs and tables, the dining rooms and passengers' cabins of the tourist class seem to transport us to a second-class waiting room. We are even more disappointed by the first class: depressing color combinations strongly dominated by violet. Earlier we observed a similar coloristic cacophony in an English hotel of high quality. Besides, there is here a relationship of seating facilities completely without imagination—one must express it thus, no composition to the room. Not a trace of any organic structure, but rather dreary functionalism without inspiration. The whole is flooded by a vast human swarm. In the tourist class there is an undefinable, amorphous mass. In the first class are well-groomed but shabby, or over-dressed older people. The obvious financial upholstery cannot offset the sagging skin. We think of our comfortable, intimate salon with its lovely pictures, in which we eat, tell stories, and laugh. The captain is gratified when upon our speedy return to his ship we make our declaration of love.

At the "Thousand Hills"

Today David drove us, together with Mr. S., to the "Thousand Hills," a jewel in Zululand among the many panoramas which we have already seen. When the car had reached the elevated vista we looked out over a highly orchestrated structure of wide-flung mountain ranges and smaller arabesques of hills. One had the impression of a fugue from which proceed new melodies, one after another. Of course, even here the typical tourist shop with its memento kitsch was not lacking. But it was early and the tourist trade had not yet started. A large sign saying that one must not miss a visit to the nearby Zulu village to experience "the natural life and the original dances" of the aborigines again put us in the gullible role of the tourist before whom a lucrative, routine show is presented. But that also is part of present-day Africa, at least in the regions visited by tourists, and that is what we are in now. Those who know the country strengthen us in the hope that on our further journey toward the east we shall meet with the wild and still unaffected Africa.

In any case, a certain curiosity overcame our aversion to the sign. Of course, we were a bit embarrassed and assured one another that we, of course, saw through the fakery but that we did not want to shut our eyes to the Africa spoiled by tourists, and so forth. Then after we had bought our tickets and without warning (at this time of day probably no one was expected) turned the corner in the neighborhood of the village, we saw several girls quickly tearing their tattered shirts from their bodies. It was, you see, rather cool and without clothing it would have been uncomfortable for them. Quick as a flash, two wives of the chief and several daughters were standing before us without anything on top. One could tell from first glance that the older women were good nourishers—or at least had been—while the young ones were plump and firm. The oldest member of the tribe greeted us in a great Zulu costume with the routine behavior of a master of ceremonies used to tourists, and immediately the older women beat the drums while the girls and the small children began to dance and sing. The young children were comical, while the older ones made a noticeable effort to overcome a certain listlessness. Their pleasure in the dance blossomed only after we filled their outstretched palms with coins and candy.

When we crept into the smoky village, we soon discovered what had whisked in there ahead of us so lightning fast: by a charcoal fire sat a young girl who held a tiny doll-like infant in her arms. Here an idyll had been constructed for just the right moment. Even though we knew this, we could not completely escape the emotion which had been intended. At least it was well done; and since the material was a bit of human innocence, it had a stronger effect than the skepticism of the enlightened and sharp-eyed. But then the old man began in a sing-song tone—he sounded like a phonograph record—to explain the details to us, showing us the divided wooden block which served him and his presently chosen wife as a pillow. And again it was impossible not to be overcome by disgust with this "nature in retirement" so spoiled by tourism. When Mr. S. asked the old man where he kept his sons, since he certainly must have succeeded in begetting not only these charming daughters, the old man was for a moment completely nonplused. It was as if the question had been asked of a programmed tape. Only after his mechanism had obviously clicked and the grinding in the switch system of his brain had been brought under control came the uncertain answer that they were working in the village. At this point Africa seemed to us almost an outgrowth of the civilization at home. Yet, even under the dreary and artificial veneer, something strange and distant was calling to us, something which existed yet as unfalsified reality somewhere on this continent. We wondered if we would ever meet it on our journey.

A visit with Dr. Haape

The visit with Dr. Haape yesterday was probably the high point of our trip up to now. It is difficult to describe how fantastic was the meeting with this man; with his family, his house, his life's work, and his thoughts which seemed to gush forth like a freshet. Our doctor friend in Hamburg, Professor Zukschwerdt, who had been imprisoned with Dr. Haape, had already told us marvelous things about him. Now, in some wonderful manner, he had heard of my presence in Durban and had immediately invited us to his home. Mrs. A., a charming, lively, older lady, the widow of a German sea officer, and now active for a long time here as a ceramics teacher, brought us, together with the captain, to the enchanted mountain hideaway where Dr. Haape, his wife, and his sixteen-year-old son Hans live. He came toward us beaming, a powerful man who immediately filled the entire scene. His magnificent head bespoke at one and the same time love of action, an intimate attachment with the earth, and intellect; his open laborer's shirt suggested someone who had just come in from plowing. "All this here I designed myself and with my boys built completely," he said, not without pride and with an all-inclusive sweep of his arm.

We are somewhat stunned, for before us rises up out of the forest a mighty castle with heavy, turreted walls of square-cut stones. "A crusader's castle under palms—I had something like that in mind. The thick walls, you know, are not only romanticism from the Middle Ages, they are also practical and keep the heat away. I need no such modern stuff as air-conditioning."

The rather large swimming pool, also formed from solid granite, has a peculiar oval form undulating in curves. He gestures with his hand at the wavy circular line: "That is supposed to represent Einstein's theory of relativity—finite but unlimited."

But more important for him than what we see here before us is the final image existing in his planning mind. Springing about from one place to another, he is able to describe it so breathtakingly that we actually seem to see the concluded work before us.

Within, we are received by the mistress of the castle. Her Austrian charm is at home even in this foreign setting. For many years a prized soloist of the Stuttgart State Opera, she has sung upon many other stages of the world as well. Son Hans hangs on his father's every word as he narrates or discusses—a touching, and in our latitude, no longer a common scene.

The interior rooms fit the castellated character of the house without the fatal impression of imitation. While the original "signature" of the builder and owner precludes the existence of stylistic purism, it assures comfort and livability and a certain personal note in the atmosphere. The house has fine guest rooms and friends are obviously very welcome here. The master of the house, an "oral" person for whom conversation is an element of life, needs communication and response. And the warmth of the great fireplace behind the heavy walls, around which we now gather, encourages discussion.

I feel that the story of how Dr. Haape came to Africa would perhaps spark him to tell us more about himself, all the more so since the name Zukschwerdt awakens his memories. He relates then that he had been a doctor, had studied psychology, and had even earned a Ph.D. (The latter came out by chance when he quoted Schopenhauer and Kant, and I mentioned that these authors were not much read by medical students.) During the war he was a medic and one of the most decorated physicians of the German armed forces. Later his son brings out the ragged uniform of the Russia campaign which he still keeps. Here in deepest Africa it has the effect of a ghostly apparition.

When he came back from imprisonment in 1952, Germany was repugnant to him for many reasons, above all because of the denazification (although he himself was not affected by it). On an exploratory trip he discovered this sequestered area, purchased it, and sent for his family. But rather than study the three more years necessary to be allowed to practice medicine here, he at first organized a plastics factory. Initially it flourished but later had to be given up. Now, under the business guidance of his wife, who is just as versatile as he, he makes fritters, which he sells in his own chain of stores.

But this somewhat adventurous history of his occupations marks only the surface of his life. Any one of the interests he designates as his hobbies could fill the life of one man. The walls are covered with his pictures, the style of which is as original and inimitable as he is himself. There are portrait drawings, often in charcoal or pencil, and also some portfolios of "watercolors" painted during his imprisonment with colors he "manufactured" himself under the most primitive conditions. For me the portraits of Russian farmers and two old men who are telling a joke remain unforgettable; their merriment is so infectious one has to join in their laughter involuntarily. The picture of an East Prussian shepherd radiates an ambiguous, melancholy wisdom that causes one to shiver. But most of all I remember a Russian youth whose wide-eyed glance mirrors the visionary gleam of an anticipated future, while it shows at the same time the decisiveness of the man of action who can seize this future. Whatever is able to mobilize a revolution of spirit, fantasy, and intention is brilliantly depicted in this one picture.

I am sorry that the charisma of this artist streams forth only in occasional creative moods, that art is not the real theme of his life. Presently, for example, he is not drawing or painting. Something else is in the works: he is composing an opera and writing the libretto himself. When he gives me a look at the voluminous manuscript, the conversation turns to the earlier work of his wife and her farewell from the stage. But then it turns out that they both have "done" opera here in Africa too. With the help of newspaper clippings and opera programs they relate how Dr. Haape founded an opera as a producer and director and presented

The Marriage of Figaro, Madame Butterfly, Tales of Hoffman, and others. He has also written a book about his experiences as a doctor at the front which has been much read in Anglo-Saxon countries.

That Dr. H. often heard me lecture in Stuttgart and knows my qualifications gives us, in addition to the rich palette of his life themes, additional starting points for lively and wide-ranging conversation which after many hours is still not exhausted. Personalities like his, whose basic nature can only develop in a free and open country outside all artificiality, narrowness, and boundaries of recent civilization, can scarcely still be found in Europe. I know of no one at home who would be comparable to this wild mountain spirit. Our conversation is as multifaceted as the man. It swings back and forth from graphic narrative and bubbling jollity to debates over philosophical and theological subjects. Also his sure faith in grace is no Christian epigonism but is rooted in personal experience.

The mentality and character of the black people

I must in the course of the hours absolutely find out how this clever man, free of prejudice and now deeply rooted in Africa, thinks concerning the problems with which I have been struggling here and which have been skirted in so many deadend conversations up to now.

I tell him what was reported to me by a black surgeon who emigrated because he could no longer bear the indignity of his situation. Although this man was a recognized, first-class expert, he could, so it was reported to me, get only half as much as was earned by the lowest white assistant. Dr. Haape does not consider such a grotesque circumstance completely impossible, but mentions in agreement with many others with whom I spoke that, on the other hand, enormous amounts were being spent for raising the social and educational levels of the Africans and that their living standard in the Union was also higher than in any other African country.

This remark occasions my next question, one which is now almost a part of my repertoire and which has unleashed so many stormy debates and controversies. It is the question whether the inferior position of the black man is constitutionally determined, and accordingly unchangeable, or whether it is based upon the historical situation and therefore can be surmounted. The long monologue with which Dr. Haape answers and which we interrupt only now and then with questions, demurring comments or affirmations, not only shows that he has often struggled mightily with these problems, but that the psychologically schooled eye of the physician allows him to see more than the average observer.

"The most important thing," he begins, "is the simple fact that with the Africans—notwithstanding all the variations and differences of tribes which still exist—we are dealing with a different *type* of human being."

"As far as I am concerned," I respond immediately, "the question is, precisely upon what difference is this based? I never do get a clear answer to *this* question. Hasn't the white rulership consciously maintained the black men in their primitivity in order to make servants of them—even without slavery? On the other hand, this explanation seems too easy for me. Robert Ruark, whose Africa novel *The Uhuru* I am just now reading, has one of his characters, certainly not without justice, ask the question: 'How much progress can you determine among your faithful, solid blacks in the last two hundred years? How much progress have you seen in Haiti, which has been black and free for over one hundred and sixty years? How much progress have you seen in Ethiopia, which has been black and free for three thousand years?' The African," I add, "never invented a wheel. Doesn't that indicate that this people is actually historically lacking in ability—and to be sure that this is not only an historical matter but is based upon an inherent deficiency? I would be really happy if you could free me from this lack of clarity and could disprove the idea of a so-called natural inferiority. Upon the solution of this question depend, indeed, not only the plans which must be made for the future history of this continent, but also the justifiability of certain political programs, for example, the thesis of South African apartheid."

Dr. Haape says cautiously: "Of course, no one knows the ultimate answer to that. Only one thing is certain—and that is unfortunately negative. The inferiority in comparison with the white ruling class is quite certainly not only to be explained historically by the head start in civilization of the whites and by clever political manipulations. I can only come back again to my thesis that, in any case, we are here dealing with a totally different type of human being."

"If this difference, however, is not to be based upon historical development, treatment, and education, then I am curious to know how you intend to convince us of the fact."

"Don't believe that I am one of those," responds Dr. Haape, "who has the point of view that the word *difference* is only the equivalent of *inferiority*. I don't intend a value judgment. The black man is simply formed by completely different climatic conditions. There is no winter for which he must prepare. There is always something to eat—coconuts, bananas, wild game. Thus he lives, as a child, for the moment and is filled by it. The European, on the other hand, has been conditioned by the change of seasons, and by many other things, to planning, to thinking for the future. And that which you have just called historical capability is associated to a great extent with the relationship to time: one learns from the past, from his tradition, and asserts himself in the present by making past experiences fruitful for future planning.

73

And now, please consider what it means in the relationship to time, and thereby in historical capability, if the conditions of nature allow the African to be absorbed in the moment."

"I see what you mean," I concur, "and it reminds me of Toynbee's thesis that a people only attains its historical role by being confronted with challenges—whether by a hostile natural environment or by the threats of neighbors—and reacting to them. These creative challenges have obviously not been the lot of the black man—at least until now."

"But how should it be possible for that to be different in the future?" one lady objects. "After all, human nature remains the same." And thus the actual difficulty and futility of the problem comes out. Dr. Haape does not take up the question, probably because he does not wish to see the difference of the black man only in a negative aspect, but also because he wishes to emphasize a factor he considers more important.

"We can only admire the Africans," he says, "when we think of the resourcefulness of their legends, of the elementary originality of their song, of the rhythm and enigma of their dances. It is no accident that the tired and exploited civilized peoples come here to borrow and to import something from the jungle to their asphalt."

"But doesn't that have an obverse side," asks the captain, "if this type of talent incapacitates them for those things which determine our civilization: for planning, sober calculation, contriving, programming, and so forth?"

"That is indeed the other side of the coin," answers Dr. Haape. "The black man in general has no ability for abstraction. I have made systematic tests with them. They seem—aside from the usual exceptions—simply not able to think mathematically. They are not able to draw squares and right angles. They do, on the other hand, succeed with circles. It is not accidental that their huts are built round."

"That agrees remarkably"—I apologize for interrupting— "with some experiences and observations which our fellow passenger, Mrs. Sch., from Windhuk, reported to us. She said the black had simply a different manner of seeing: their Ovambo serving girl absolutely could not lay a tablecloth straight on the table except in the rooms where the lines of the carpet flooring could be used as a guide. When the crookedness was called to the attention of the girl, she could only stare uncomprehendingly; she just did not see it. But she could immediately see a tiny beetle in a distant corner of the room when we could not see it. Mrs. Sch. even asserted that ophthalmologists had determined that the paralax in the lens of the eye of blacks was differently structured and responsible for their faulty apprehension of angles."

Here Dr. Haape shook his head somewhat skeptically and left undecided the question whether the mentioned geometrical peculiarities of the Africans were physiologically determined or caused by their environment and therefore also correctable. "Where would the black, in his jungle or in the hills, come across a straight line or a right angle?" he countered. "When you buy a Makande sculpture in East Africa, you will find out that the underside is not planed flat. It sits somewhat unsteadily on your table and must be accordingly corrected. Is this because these artists— and there are real artists among them—could not see a level surface and cut it? No, there is a much more simple reason. Since they have no tables, they place their figures in the dust of the ground, and that itself is not level."

Meanwhile Mrs. Haape has served a highly tasty meat pastry. We don't go to the table, but take the plates upon our knees. Mrs. A., who until now has listened silently, asks the master of the house to tell still more about the "differentness" of the native mentality. This is indeed a fascinating theme for us—not only because of the problems presented by it but for reasons of a certain romanticism. We are still in a highly civilized and ostensibly European country. The subject of differentness, however, turns our gaze to that distant, strange Africa, far removed from our understanding, which we still want to meet. It doesn't need to be so mysteriously removed from our understanding as the horrible ceremonies of Ruark's Kikuyu Mau Mau in Kenya. Yet I am almost more interested in the everyday psychological symptoms such as white South Africans notice in their dealings with the natives.

What was not considered in developmental aid

"I will gladly give you some examples," begins Dr. Haape at the instance of Mrs. A, "by which it recently became clear to me in what another world of thought and imagination our black brothers live here. In this neighborhood a short time ago a native hut burned down. The white farmer for whom the native family worked was sympathetic to their loss and gave the head of the family money for a new hut and furnishings. A short time afterwards the farmer's house burned down. It turned out that the originator of this fire was the same man who had been the recipient of the farmer's largesse. When questioned why he had done it, the guilty man said, 'My master gave me a hut as a gift. I could not see the reason for this. Therefore he must have had a bad conscience toward me. He certainly must have done something to me or misused me, even if I don't know it. Therefore I revenged myself.' "

After this astounding story, L. reminds me of the conversation we had with an Englishman on board ship. He told us that in the Bantu language there was no word for "thank you." This information, indeed, corresponds with what was just reported. The African—at least those we are talking about here—obviously has in his mentality no room for something given selflessly and without reason. When he encounters something like this he cannot understand it and thus seeks a motive, some dark intention—or a bad conscience from which one seeks to free himself.

Dr. Haape confirms this and adds: "You can imagine what the effect is upon natives when white tourists give them excessive tips. In their naïveté they probably think their generosity is producing gratitude. But it really encourages the question: What does the white man mean by this? Why does he want to bring me to my knees? Or, what bad thing has he done from which he seeks to excuse himself?"

At this point an expostulation escapes the captain: "Good heavens, what does all this mean for our developmental help!"

"Indeed," interjects Dr. Haape immediately, "you have just touched a nerve which our well-meaning politicians at home—but also in America and the other European countries—probably think too little about. For these politicians, developmental help is either a political move (to eliminate the general unrest and ideological pitfalls caused by mass suffering); economic, to gain new consumers for industrial products, to open up new markets, and thereby to increase buying power; or a philanthropical motive; or all three together. Only *one* factor is, as a rule, forgotten: the psychological one. One does not consider that the native mentality does not comprehend a gift. Now, I am naturally not so naive as to think that developmental help is offered from purely unselfish motives, and I have just named some very palpable, calculated aims and calculating people. But to me there is too much talk about moral and humanitarian duty to the Africans, about the social obligations of the rich to the poor people, and similar eyewash. The people here take all that the wrong way, and they interpret it only as an expression of a bad conscience which the white man suffers on account of his colonial exploitation. But aside from this, too, developmental help is a broad field. People willing to help are needed much more than the industrial investments for which the Africans won't be ready for a long time. And one would have to watch very closely down what dark canals great sums of money might disappear."

Frau Haape comments that we will be together for too short a time to exhaust our energies upon this unfathomable theme. She guesses our interest correctly when she suggests her husband should tell us something more of his experiences among the Africans when they are left to themselves.

"We experienced that on a small scale a few years ago," relates Dr. Haape, "when a monastery was erected in our region with native monks and a black abbot. It was provided with a complete agricultural operation—cattle, tools, and considerable wooded territory. After a few years everything was hopelessly run down: the cattle sick and decimated, the trees cut down, the living quarters and stalls in ruin. Then white padres and lay brothers again had to be sent in to set the damage right. And it is also like that on a large scale: where there are decolonized black governments, trade and exchange decline and the people earn much less than before. Blacks can live satisfactorily only when they are under the knout of a native tyranny, which systematizes dispositions and brings to bear the necessary pressure to keep them at work. But even this works—at least at the present time—only when the black rulers have white advisors at their disposal to take care of the organization. Notice when you come to East Africa how much better everything works in Kenya than in Tanganyika. You will see this in the harbors themselves. And what is the reason? Solely the fact that in Kenya, thanks to the wisdom of the president, whites are always employed at the control mechanisms."

"Up to now we have spoken of the distance and the difference between the whites and blacks," I resume. "Indeed our question was aimed at this. But is it not all too generalized and simplistic when we speak of *the* black, *the* African? Is there such a thing at all? Obviously there exists within the Africans themselves considerable differences of ability and development—distances scarcely less than those between black and white—which produce corresponding apartheid tendencies among the Africans also. During my stay in the southwest ten years ago, for instance, a certain Herero who was employed as a bus driver refused to transport Ovambos in his conveyance or to fill in for their driver who was ill. This was indeed apartheid in its purest form, and this tribal phariseeism might even be greater than the arrogance of the white race toward the black."

"To be sure," answers our host, "these intra-African differentiations and differences make the racial problems very much more difficult. But much would be gained if at least one very simple thing were realized which is usually not noticed because of purely humanitarian daydreaming through ideologically fogged glasses: that one is dealing here with people of a completely different type, and not merely with mini-Europeans whom one only needs to enlarge to the fully developed form of a normal European."

Thus the conversation returns to the point where it began. Meanwhile it has become very late. The bottles are empty and the fire in the hearth has become a bed of glowing coals. We are tired. The hours here have been spent in considerable excitement, and it is quite a long way to the ship.

The heartiness of the farewell and the hope for another meeting aboard the *Tanganyika* do not alter the fact that I leave this fine and fulfilling round of conversation in deep perplexity. On the drive back to the ship we talk about it. The decisive questions seem to us more insoluble than ever. The deeper one penetrates, the more unfathomable everything becomes. We have lost our naïve self-assuredness. Our increasing "enlightenment" does not lead to clarity but creates chain reactions of new questions, and the end is not in sight. To be sure, Dr. Haape had some answers. But isn't even this imposing and independent spirit influenced by the trends of South African thinking? Will not much appear quite differently to us when we come to the East Coast, to Mozambique, Tanzania, and Kenya? Or will the open questions continue to extend themselves infinitely?

When we fondly board the brightly lighted ship, upon which the loading work continues even at night, the torturing questions begin to quieten for the moment. We discuss what will happen tomorrow evening. The anticipation of coming things presses to the foreground. Curiosity is a good therapy for brooding.

Mozambique

From the "waiting room" just out of the harbor where we lay at anchor since yesterday afternoon, we moved on to the pier this morning of my birthday. Seldom have I celebrated it so pleasantly. Someone remarks that we have become a large family. Just outside my room I was greeted by a large "Happy Birthday" sign which had been painted by little Sprat. She also found some very pretty cuff links for me in Durban which I absolutely must wear today. From the captain I received a bouquet, and among the other gifts was a large Zulu doll which will certainly mean complete bliss for my little granddaughter. The ship's cook has baked a cake creation which we, even in our larger circle, and in spite of mutual encouragement, cannot completely consume. According to my usual fate, this day also brings an endlessly long telegram from Hamburg which has to do with joyless university matters and must be answered immediately.

The harbor activity is immeasurably more lively—more Southern, so to speak—than the more systematic, relaxed and subdued work of the South African loaders. We all notice it immediately. An older white man who oversees the unloading at the stern particularly fascinates us. He gives his signals with gigantic temperament to the crane operator. Head, arms, and trunk are like a musical conductor gone wild in convulsive activity, now encouraging, now subduing. For every vertical or horizontal change of direction he has a special bird call which he twitters and whistles. At the same time he urges the black stevedores on with a gigantic roar of voice, dreadfully scolding and again laughing wildly, while they jump and seize the crates, grinning and joking all the while. He seems to be a popular foreman, because he simultaneously entertains and supervises loading operations with care. Life here is highly temperamental and dynamic, combining southern vitality with the purposefulness that still functions as a trademark of the once so stormy Portuguese rule.

In this heat it is unbelievable to me with what speed and cheerful devotion the blacks scoop the large containers of manganese and clay out of the wagons, then heave them up and unload the contents into the holds with a sound like thunder. The gigantic clouds of dust settle in crusts on their sweat-dampened bodies. When the long railway cars come, piled high with their massive loads, one can scarcely imagine how they will be accommodated. But then they are empty in a wink. In one of the vacant cars I see an African leaning against the wall in the deep sleep of exhaustion. When the car is suddenly shunted too violently and strikes another with a powerful bang, he only starts up momentarily, looks about, surprised, and then immediately goes to sleep again. One of us would have suffered a concussion. To my question why no machines are used for this man-killing work but as in the old times everything is done by hand, the captain opines it is probably feared that people would be put out of work by the machines. Besides, manpower is very cheap here.

In a tour through the city we admire the magnificent breadth of the Avenida da Republica. From a distance it is reminiscent of the Champs Élysées, and we seek to gain a panoramic view of land and sea from the roof of a seventeen-story skyscraper. Mr. M., a businessman who lives here, accompanies us. His comments add to our impressions and help us see more deeply and, at the same time, more "symbolically." The comparison with South Africa occurs to us immediately, since here there is no apartheid. The signs "For Whites Only" on buses, restrooms, box offices, and benches are completely absent. And yet it is not to be concealed from us, that, except for well-dressed Indian families with many children, one really meets only whites in the cafes and restaurants. Africans are seen only in positions of service: as waiters, chauffeurs, shoe-shine boys, street workers. Great swarms of them also sell innumerable items on the streets.

Among the countless beggars and street vendors we notice some who are horribly crippled. As we sit in front of a cafe along the street to observe the colorful life and to refresh ourselves with ice-cold orange juice, a lottery vendor with bizarrely crippled legs creeps on all fours from table to table reaching up his merchandise with pleading glances. The complete indifference and disregard with which people reject him bothers me greatly at first. I cannot understand why others are so little touched by this suffering human creature. But during the course of the day I notice how something changes within me, and I again experience what occurred in East Asia: one simply would never have been able to get rid of the hordes of running and begging children if he paid the slightest attention to them, and (as I at first did) gave them candy. Disregard is a type of self-defense without which one would be lost. If I were always to remain here, this nonchalance certainly would become second nature with me too. As a mere visitor, however, one must struggle with contradictory feelings and manifold embarrassments. How is one, as a Christian, to come to terms with this? The simplest questions are often more difficult than the deepest problems of high theology. Life is truly a complicated undertaking, if one is not simply to play dead like an animal. As travelers just arrived from South Africa, we naturally keep our eyes open to see what form the relationship of the races takes here where there is no legal apartheid. To be sure, since people are not artificially kept apart, they seem to mix together in a much less prejudiced way.

Nevertheless, there was obviously a type of latent and unofficial apartheid here—at any rate a distinct boundary between white and black—and it would be peculiar if a certain social distance were not connected with it. When we ask Mr. M. about this it turns out our earlier impression is correct; things are different, but also somewhat more involved than in South Africa. "Here too there is a, so-to-speak, 'naturally' developed apartheid," explains Mr. M., "but it is less a racial than a social phenomenon. It affects the blacks especially in that they represent at the same time the socially lower class and thus automatically are separated from the 'Europeans.' "

"But these things are nevertheless not legally determined as in South Africa?" I ask.

"Yes and no. In any case, differently. The Portuguese, who, of course, do not consider Mozambique a colony but an 'overseas province' and include it in their own legal structure, have found a very clever solution: whoever cannot read and write, owns nothing, and thus is not a taxpayer, does not have the status of a Portuguese citizen. This includes most of the Africans. Therefore it is an effective socio-political apartheid! But it does not include *only* blacks. A substantial contingent of whites does not meet the requirements of citizenship and can therefore not vote either."

I ask if this does not cause social resentment, whether the privileged are not envied their citizenship, and whether this is not a source of contention.

"This is true only within certain limits," he answers, "and I have never noticed anything in the way of class struggles in this area. The reason is quite simple: if one is a free, privileged citizen, he must pay taxes. And this prospect naturally checks such ambitions."

We do not have the impression—and others confirm this later—that the class difference between white and black is less here than in South Africa. In fact, the living standard of the black seems rather to be considerably lower. Here also, then, the problem of the coexistence of different races presents itself in unallayed sharpness. My old question as to whether the subordination of the black race is biologically or historically determined, of course, appears still more confusing here because the racial question forms a quite insoluble complex with the social. Nevertheless it is possible that capable individuals among the Africans can rise to higher positions and that the whites in their official capacity (privately, probably less) associate with them in an uninhibited manner as with their own kind. As we learn, the primacy of *social* hierarchies also is to be seen in the manner in which more highly placed Africans look down with disdain upon the laborers and illiterates of their race and act in a very lordly manner toward them. The self-confidence of the successful ones produces a new variant of apartheid—not dissimilar to the previously mentioned form which showed itself in the arrogance of supposedly superior tribes, for instance, in the disdain of the Hereros toward the Ovambos.

I have a dreadful toothache and want to have the offender pulled. Consultations with visitors who know the circumstances here cause me to recoil from a visit to the consulting rooms. I am told real horror stories about the hospitals and dentists. Whoever can afford it flies from here to Johannesburg to have his teeth taken care of or to be operated upon, so I decide to fight the inflammation with pain pills and penicillin. And in case of emergency, so I am assured, there is a pair of pliers on board and strong men to manipulate them. The infernal heat in the black limousine where I protect my ailing jaw from drafts makes me so uncomfortable that I often forget the toothache and am thus able to remember some impressions: the many streets laid out like boulevards, the glowing rows of royal poinciana trees, the drunken exuberance of the vegetation in the suburban gardens.

The Cabora-Bassa dam project
as seen from Mozambique

As an interesting architectural structure the San Antonio church particularly remains in memory. It is called the "lemon squeezer" because its concrete skeleton really reminds one of this gadget. The cathedral of Brasília immediately occurred to us because of its similar, although immeasurably more powerful, structure which also was finished only in the rough when we saw it. It impressed us as an imposing ruin which does not recall the past but points to the future. And not only have financial factors delayed its completion for many years. When we are struck with wonder that on a normal Friday morning so many people visited the San Antonio church as worshipers although there wasn't even a service, Mr. N. comments that, nevertheless, attendance has recently declined considerably. I can scarcely imagine how bitterly received here was the resolution of the Ecumenical Council to give financial support to the "freedom fighters" of Tanzania. I remark that this causes both churches to be thrown into the same pot, so that the Catholics also have to suffer. On the northern boundary of Mozambique, people had to fight hard and often with heavy losses against the attacking "Maoists" who were infiltrating as partisans, and they simply could not understand that the church had made iself an ally in these attacks. The "Maoist" freedom fighters had threatened to postpone their decisive blow until the giant project of the Cabora-Bassa Dam was half finished, so that they could then blow it up, along with its ten thousands of construction workers. The talk here was that "Mao and the church" (!) had planned this work of destruction!

Although I myself definitely disapprove the resolution of the Ecumenical Council, nevertheless, in order to induce further information and also to test the degree of critical judgment, I launch a small argumentative attack on Mr. N. and later on two visitors on board. My question is: "What would you say to the arguments of the radical left in Germany that developmental measures of the proportions of this dam benefited a governmental system considered colonialistic, and that this questionable governmental system was strengthened thereby?" The answer is not completely satisfying. One who is immediately entangled in acute conflicts perhaps does not have sufficient breathing room for continuing considerations of basic principles. I will probably be confronted with this problem even more often on my further travels, and perhaps we will come then to more deeply reaching discussions. The first reaction to my question is, in both conversations, remarkably similar. Any thorough help, so my interlocutors say, will naturally at first be to the benefit of the regime which at that time finds itself in power. But such a giant project as the Cabora-Bassa Dam, which transforms the entire landscape, creates a great industrial area, and revolutionizes the economical structure of this country from the ground up, is naturally a matter to be viewed in the long term and will outlast the present constellations of power. At present, I am told, electrical power in Mozambique is probably the most expensive in the world. It must be brought in from far away in a complicated and expensive manner. But after construction of the dam, Mozambique will be among the countries which produce the most inexpensive electricity. It does not take a very penetrating mind, they say, to imagine what this reduction in price and the reformation of the economic and social structure occasioned by it would mean for precisely the poorer levels of the population.

This evening, when the heat has lessened and a soft breeze at least gives the illusion of occasional coolness, an English couple (Mr. R. represents the German Africa lines here) has invited the captain and us to dinner. We drive to a restaurant on the beach of the Costa del Sol and allow ourselves to be fanned by the sea breeze on the great crowded terrace. For supper there is a famous Lourenço-Marques dish: crabs and prawns, a type of lobster which one shells with the hands and eats in the same way. The table is set only for the sake of convention. During the meal we are given bowls with lemon slices floating in warm water so that we can clean our grease-dripping hands. More and more hot plates with the delicate fruits of the sea are brought in, while servant boys clear away the scraps. A bitter mocha brings to a close the joys of the dining table and again makes us sufficiently capable on the drive back to the ship of coping with the impressions of the Lourenço's Repperbahn. Under the harsh, glimmering, illuminated advertisements, the *dolce vita* of those who have been castaways is acted out, and I think with concern of the many young faces who experience on land nothing other than this type of "adventure." The black ladies of the night rule the field. Their faces are, to some extent, just as shocking as their often fabulously powerful and projecting anatomies, of which one has the impression that the weight of the upper front side is only balanced by a corresponding counterweight astern. Mr. R. explains the mad human swarm to us—particularly large on weekends—by the fact that bright hordes of South Africans come here in order to revel in a way which is denied to them under apartheid at home.

Back on the ship we close the day by entertaining one another with stories about our experiences on land.

**Lourenco Marques
December 5**

In the morning the car fetches us for a further drive into the surrounding areas. Past lonely native dwellings consisting only of disheveled walls made of leaves—they do not even in the least degree deserve the name of huts—we come finally to the Villa Luisa. There a motorboat is waiting to take us on a one-hour journey up river to a place where one can see the hippopotamuses. As we drive past deserted, treeless riverbanks with only here and there a few bushes, we meet now and then small rowboats with fishermen. Here they throw out their nets in exactly as primitive a manner as in biblical times. Only seldom do we see a lonely fisherman's hut on the banks. Then, near a small island, the hippopotamuses actually emerge. When their gigantic bodies are under water and only the heads are visible, one sees real horse-faces. There is the impression of suddenly being transported into the world of fable where the animal figures of ancient times are not only bound to their "natural" environment but sovereignly traverse the elements of air, earth, water, and fire. As soon as our helmsman sounds the boat's horn, these curious creatures come up to investigate what strange beast of legendary times is howling so energetically. They approach so very near to us and have such a familiar and pet-like manner that we suddenly catch ourselves waving to them. We almost want to feed them sugar cubes.

In the afternoon we could not bathe in the ocean because of the ebb and also because the sand is burning hot, so we go to a large modern swimming pool. What pleasure awaits us here is not furnished by the bathtub-warm water, but by the noisy, swarming folk festival which unfolds all around us. All shades of skin teem in a potpourri; of apartheid there is really nothing to be seen. One cannot rightly tell what sounds louder in the ears: the dance music from the loudspeaker, which actually creates waves, or the shrieks of joy of the young people who are chasing, scuffling, and continually egging each other on.

In the terrace restaurant which lies directly at the water's edge, a wedding is being celebrated. The young people dance wildly and tirelessly in the oven-like heat, with all the textiles of civilization: in collars, neckties, long-sleeved shirts soaked with perspiration, and many even in good jackets. The dressing rooms are full of dirt and disorder. In the shower only one spigot functions and only halfway at that. It is besieged. When I enter the room everyone courteously makes way immediately, engaging in all kinds of horseplay until I finish—a cheerful little people for whom the foreigner is a welcome change.

Later on the street we meet the captain, who persuades us instead of eating on the ship to stage a sequel to yesterday's lobster feast. Mr. S. and I are wearing only short pants and short sleeves, not even socks, because of the heat and our intention to swim. But in our travel book it says that the restaurants in this land are somewhat formal. It is not at all as bad as that, the captain assures us. People would think we are Rhodesians, and so they probably do.

Uninvited guests at a Muslim wedding

While we are devoting ourselves to gustatory bliss we observe a constantly increasing crowd and a rising confusion of voices in front of an adjacent school. The waiters tell us that an Arabian Muslim wedding is taking place there. Already large caravans of cars have roared past us with deafening horns and sirens. That was the overture, and now, instead of the horns, human mouths are making the uproar. Among Europeans there is a restrained attention even in front of the church when a bridal pair drives up with its retinue or comes out of the portal, and then it is mostly older women who indulge in wistful memories or admire the clothes. All the while it is almost as silent as in the church itself. Here, however, the entire quarter of the city seems to have come together and children make up the noisy majority of the spectators.

When we are finished with the meal and want to stretch our legs a bit, we stroll to the center of the happenings and mingle among the army of excitedly chattering old people and shouting, chasing children. Probably we betray our interest when we stretch our necks a little to see what is happening. Presently a courteous young man in a well-cut safari suit approaches us— later it turns out he is the brother of the bride—and in English invites us to come nearer and accompany him into the house. I am considerably embarrassed in my slightly glorified bathing outfit. It has always been one of my occasional nightmares to suddenly pop up in a society of formally dressed people in my nightshirt, and here I seem to be coming quite close to that. Mr. S., however, an acquisiteur by profession—I have translated that for him as a "smiler"—has long since overcome inhibitions of this sort in his job and is already halfway up the steps. Thus we follow *nolens volens* and even the much more genteelly dressed captain gives himself a shove and enters.

We are then brought into the large school auditorium filled with people. When L. notices that it is a gathering of men only, she starts backward and wants to take flight. But the young man reassures her: as an out-of-town guest—he politely avoids the word *tourist*—she may also take part. Still, she tried to appear very small in this crowded room of men.

On the podium sits a large circle of highly impressive men, all in black fezzes or in white wool caps. It appears to be a mixed society of Indians and Arabians. Several of the old men give the impression of a foregathering of patriarchs from the Old Testament: distinctive, sharply profiled heads with great well-groomed beards. These are probably the dignitaries of the Muslim community. The high priest in the center, completely clothed in white, is the image of a distinguished Arabian sheik. Several imposing figures of this type also sit in the audience. The majority of those present, however, are by no means solemnly dressed and obviously are not in a solemn mood. People are smoking and chattering and much time passes. I keep waiting for the entrance of the bridal pair, and finally ask our young host about it. His perplexing answer is that there isn't one. The women are— probably symbolically!—one floor below, gathered with the bride and her retinue. The young man up in front, a slender figure in the midst of powerful, patriarchal figures, is the bridegroom. The day after tomorrow he must go into the military for four years and during that time his young wife will not see him.

The bride seems to be only the *object* of the ceremony. Her "yes" is without importance. Marriage is a family matter and it is arranged by men.

Suddenly the cigarettes are put out. Things are undoubtedly getting started. The high priest begins a typical singsong, familiar to us from the minarets of the mosques. Then he makes a long address which is so rich in gesture, so rhetorically masterful in crescendoes, cadences, and restrained pauses, that it is fascinating even when one understands nothing and only occasionally catches a familiar name like that of Abraham.

Now the fathers of the bride and bridegroom and other worthy men are asked a question, in answer to which they nod their heads and write their signatures. The bridegroom and his father are bedecked with a great load of colorful garlands, which they take off from time to time in order to receive new ones. Finally, short speeches are made and letters of good wishes are read aloud. Some of the speakers, among them an old, frail man who nevertheless speaks in a fiery manner, are greeted and thanked with wild applause. Almost all of them seem to be born rhetoricians. But one young man, perhaps a fraternity brother of the bridegroom, is not well practiced in the art of extemporaneous speaking and, besides, he cannot find his manuscript. While on the podium he digs hectically in all his pockets and does a real St. Vitus dance of embarrassment, all the while inundated by laughter from the audience. When he finally locates his notes, he calmly reads the prepared sentences aloud.

After a short religious closing ceremony, everything suddenly breaks up and our new acquaintance leads us to the lower floor where the women are. There, at the first glance, everything looks incomparably more festive. The splendid Indian festive saris are a magnificent palette of colors. The women sit there silently in their assembly, which is just as large. As we are led in, goosebumps rise on my bare calves in the midst of this festive brilliance because all eyes have fixed themselves on us with interest. Meanwhile, our escort has increased by a number of young men, and they do not at all want us to have only a fleeting glance at the assembly hall. We must also admire the bride and are therefore thrust forward to the center of the front part of the hall. There we see her dressed exactly as our brides are dressed, sitting in solitary splendor upon the stage. The lovely, eighteen-year-old creature is obviously intimidated and exhausted by being stared at by the mutely waiting crowd. Somewhat troubled, she looks at us, for now other and even more unfamiliar eyes are directed at her. Next to her sit two bridesmaids who incessantly cool her with fans.

As part of the farewell, which proceeds in a very hearty manner, we receive, like all the guests, small packages of candy. This, then, was something not planned for tourists, but real life that we have encountered. As so often happens, the most beautiful things are those that we blunder into unexpectedly.

Lourenco Marques
December 6

The clouds of dust from the loading of manganese gradually drift away. We sit in the cool rooms of the ship and watch with unbelief the black stevedores doing this difficult dirty work in 41° C. humid heat. What sort of bigwigs we are! With this somewhat rotten feeling it does me good to remember that I was able to get along on the East Asia trip in similar heat on a ship with no air-conditioning. But even then I was no laborer, but lived on the level of a passenger. Now and then the foremen come in out of the blazing sun into our bar and gulp down cool beer. The twittering bird-man who is also here suddenly seems quiet and mild. Only his odd, chiseled physiognomy announces that he is not just anyone.

Today is the Second Sunday in Advent. I read the texts of the day so that in thought I can be with my congregation as we celebrate this solemnity of the end of the world with the deeply affecting verses of the 24th chapter of Matthew. I am particularly touched by the admonition of Jesus that the people might ask in the anguish at the end, when hell opens up and the terror of the last days is unloosed, that their flight not occur in winter. How often have people told me what these words meant to them during their flight across the snows in the Russian winter of 1944 and 1945. It could also be just as bad to have to flee in this horrible heat and not to have a sheltering shadow. These stark apocalyptic verses affect me especially now, although we are on a vacation trip. The problems of the world by which we are confronted when we see this compulsory servitude and have so many conversations that terminate with dead-ends show that chaos seethes directly under the "thin appleskin" of civilization, or—to express it in the words from the first chapter of the Bible—that the water under the firmament and the water above the firmament break through the dams erected by God and would destroy us in new floods of water or fire.

5:45 p.m.

We have just put out to sea and are now passing the Costa del Sol where we ate the day before yesterday. The captain says that we have a wind velocity of eight. This wind, however, does not cool but is rather like the breath from a furnace. The captain is somewhat concerned that the pilot will not be able to board with the waves so high. Then we would have to wait until the weather calms. We are anxious.

10:00 p.m.

The pilot has made it. He was happily hoisted up on board and received into the arms of his men on the bobbing ship.

When we went on deck after supper, a tropical storm of continually increasing vehemence broke loose and quickly subdued the unbearable heat. At the first flashes of lightning there were some "ahs" and "ohs" from those who stand captivated on the rolling bridge. Then the brightness jolted and crackled around us, vertically and horizontally and back and forth. In bizarre figures the lightning chased itself across the expanse of horizon. For moments it was overspread with such blinding brightness that we involuntarily had to duck only to be swallowed up again immediately in unfathomable darkness. I think of Haydn's *Creation*—the radiant and joyous setting of the words, "And there was light." The world seems to be newly created in stark brightness by the "spirit above the waters." Just as the lightning springs from one horizon to the other, so one's thoughts spring from the earliest beginnings to that end of the world of which the texts of the Second Coming tell: the elements melt and judgment comes.

In Beira

Beira
December 8

We have scarcely docked when I am visited by the German consul, Mr. St., a native of Hamburg, who puts himself at our disposal for information and for drives around the area. When we gladly accept his delightful offer and then moan somewhat about the temperature in the hot car, I lament that I am made extra hot by my long dress pants. Mr. St. answers that he usually goes around in shorts and had only put on long trousers today in my honor. He wanted to appear correct before me as the "diplomatic representative of the Federal Republic of Germany."

"Good heavens," I exclaim, "and I had my shorts on this morning! But when I glimpsed through the curtain and saw you so

95

completely dressed, I rushed into my room and changed into long trousers."

"So we have both been play-acting," says the consul with a smile, "and now we must bear the consequences."

On the drive through Beira, it impresses us as a highly disorganized city with no architectural character. One is scarcely past the narrow, suffocating streets swarming with people in the older part of town when suddenly, without transition, one meets with large office buildings, banks, and public buildings. Especially impressive are two modern and magnificently designed school complexes, one of which belongs to the Catholic mission. (Just as in Mozambique, the school and hospital system is chiefly run by the missions.) The modern and palatial train station seems to serve mainly symbolic purposes, for not many more than four trains per day arrive here. But Beira knows its future as a transportation crossroads, and this train station is, like the just-as-modern airport, more an indication of hoped-for and coming things than an expression of the present. On the whole, Beira is just as devoid of charm as a suburban area in the Ruhr region.

When we come upon the nearby beach it is like an emancipation. In a short while, when the Christmas vacation begins, the vast sandy coasts will fill with campers from Rhodesia, we are told. Their harbingers have already appeared. A cast-off grand hotel which went bankrupt several years ago projects itself in an eerie manner as a last offshoot of the city toward the sea. The ruined splendor of yesteryear creates an even more miserable effect than the poverty of the natives' huts. With these at least there is no incongruence between pretension and reality. Consul St., who emends and informs our observations, especially in confirming the social character of apartheid here, tells us on the drive of the missionary activity of the White Fathers. He is in active contact with them and advises them as the East African manager of the BASF, especially in questions of artificial fertilizing. At my request he drives us immediately to the area far outside of the city.

96

Visit to the mission of the White Fathers

On a flat landscape of sand and bushes, upon which a humid, sun-drenched atmosphere weighs brooding and motionless, are situated a large school building and the living areas for the padres, the brothers, and the teaching sisters. The entire area is surrounded by a great number of modest stone houses for the native catechist pupils and their families. We immediately meet young Father R. from Austria and the Upper Swabian brother, Stanislaus, under whose direction everything we see here has been built in the last years. Their greeting is thoroughly cordial and their joy about our visit unfeigned. The father wears a white linen maxi-dress, something like a nightgown, which reaches to his feet and which probably gave the order its name. The sisters are also dressed in snow white. The idea of their going about dressed in black in this heat makes one shudder!

Father R. is a radiantly fresh young man who runs this impressive work like a motor. Three years ago there was only an empty steppe here. In the struggle with his ecclesiastical superiors, who were skeptical about such adventurous initiatives, and also in hand combat with the countless other difficulties, he begged the financial means on many journeys, acquired the property, and erected a large number of buildings. While we slowly stroll from building to building and he becomes quite excited in telling the story of the gauntlet of difficulties he has had to run, I ask him what future plans he has for his self-chosen work.

His conception is clear and very plausible: In the small Diaspora congregations which jut out of the ocean of animism like tiny islands, he seeks out the most talented among the young men and brings them here with their families for a course of two years to educate them as catechists. In this time, they are to gain the capability of teaching, preaching, baptizing, performing marriages and burials. Brother Stanislaus educates them in matters of

97

agriculture while the wives learn the rudiments of child care, general hygiene, sewing, and other domestic skills from the sisters. Thus small centers can spring up in many other places where the knowledge acquired here is passed on.

The father leads us into one of the small houses which is occupied by a catechist family. The cool living room is almost empty and contains only a bench and a table. There is a conscious effort not to deluge these young Africans with civilization and thus increase their separation from village life all too greatly. An estrangement from their native milieu must be avoided, for it would make their return difficult. At the table stands a small feminine creature holding a tiny newborn infant in her arms. At first I thought the little nurse was the older sister of the baby, but it is, however, the mother who bore the child two days before. The young catechists beam at us everywhere we walk. The sullen expression which I often (often!) think I see on black faces is missing here. Do I only imagine that they "look redeemed"? I don't think so, although I am always on guard against a certain preacher mentality. Even in East Asia I could often recognize the "Christian face." What one notices here is the emancipation from dark powers which baffle our understanding. Of course, there is also the difference from those often stiff faces of many among us who are Christians in name only, of whom Nietzsche made the famous dictum that these people would look more saved if they believed in their Savior.

I like the young padre from the first moment. He shines with enthusiasm for his work and has the characteristics of a man who sacrifices himself in service. He is at the same time cheerful and unusually relaxed, without any tinge of fanaticism and not without joy in the good things of life: in table tennis, for example, in which he and the consul plan another duel.

Mr. St. asks him if he is not concerned that the young Christian families he is sending back to the Diaspora congregations could again fall under the spell of animism since they will be surrounded by heathendom there. He gives answer with great certainty, and is actually radiant as he says: "If I did not know and had not experienced that they stand firm and will stand firm, I could never have found the courage to continue this work."

His manner reminds me very much of the young Protestant missionaries with whom I visited the Herero and Ovambo preserves in the southwest over ten years ago. How differently this new generation lives and thinks than the worthy pioneer fathers who formerly blazed trails under indescribable conditions of sacrifice! Even here is visible the same decisive break between the generations as is characteristic for almost all areas of life. Formerly one spoke very directly and perhaps all too unreflectively of God and Christ without taking the heathen background into consideration and thus caused the Christian message to appear very much different from the original intent of the Master. Perhaps to the "barbarians" the god of the Christians was only a type of top deity in the hierarchy of the old familiar idols and spirits. The new faith was then only integrated into their animistic schema, and the religion of their fathers lived on under a patina of Christianity which only touched the surface. It was no wonder then that the old powers which had long been thought dead broke out of their condition of incubation again and seized anew the scepter of power which had been taken from them. They had only been subdued, not really conquered.

I was especially struck by the regeneration of heathen worship among the spiritists in Brazil: for their cult worship they had, in addition to the Christian altar, yet another "altar" with African spirit masks and figures of idols. Here Christianization had been extremely superficial and had not even made the attempt to subdue and dissolve the connections with the native religion. Since this country could be entered only by baptized Christians, it was then the custom simply to sprinkle the hordes of African slaves with a little baptismal water as they left the ship. Of course, that did not drive out the old gods; they merely coughed a little, at the most, and then enjoyed a new resurrection under Christian auspices.

99

As I already said, that was an extreme case, and matters were by no means so slovenly among the missions in Africa. But all the same, there was probably great naïveté in regard to the nature and power of animistic ideas. One preached, so to speak, not at them but rather past them. On the other hand, scientific research into primitive religions owes much to the missionaries. But this knowledge was probably too little utilized theologically and played only a small role in evangelism. Those of us who know the extraordinary efforts and sacrifice of our forebears can frankly admit this, without an undertone of pharisaical priggishness.

The young generation of missionaries regards itself much more intensively within the framework of native religious backgrounds. It seeks to encounter and mediate. It also knows the values of the pre-Christian world of religion and does not simply deny it but builds upon it. For them it is not just superstition but rather a perverted connection with the divinity, who is evident even in this distorted form.

Perhaps one could characterize this new element in evangelism in the present-day theology of the mission. The direction of the integration process has been reversed. Whereas earlier Christianity—in contradiction to the intention of its first representatives—was variously built into the religious schema of heathendom and then remained burdened as an imported novelty, today the old hierarchy of Gods and spirits is fitted into the framework of the new faith. With the dissimilarity of these beliefs, the new inner world can relate to the old one which it displaced. In Christ the other religions are not simply debased but rather fulfilled through conflict. The padre maintains that the second Vatican council gave unprecedented impulse to this purpose. It showed the way to the appreciation not only of other religions but also atheism, and to it gave impulse to understanding them in the light of Christ.

I then asked *him* my question (which has now almost become stereotyped) whether, upon the basis of his experience, he considers the primitive black tribes to be ultimately incapable of development, or whether their backwardness springs from the fact that the white colonial rulership has consciously hindered the development of their slumbering potentials. The padre's answer is different from anything which I have heard up to now from a European, even from other vital Christians. It expresses clearly the Catholic theses of the analogy of all being (*Analogia entis*). He in fact ignores my question and says merely: "We don't know what fullness of potential will be revealed when the so-called 'barbarian' discovers the dignity of his existence within Christ's field of force. Here the African is not," continues the padre, "confronted with a completely strange world, as he is in technical civilization with a world which he cannot digest. The new world of faith can really fuse with him, become a part of him; his nature can accept it."

This hope of faith which actually seems to bubble forth from the young priest affects me deeply with its magnificence and at the same time makes me feel quite humble. Once again the generation gap occurs to me. Obviously, the padre does not expect that the conversion will set a melting pot process in motion which will finally produce a type of *doppelgänger* of the European Christian and at the same time an alienated image of the former "savage." No, what will finally be accomplished by this miracle of spirit is not even to be seen in its outlines today. It can be the creation of a new being which even our boldest fancies cannot imagine. Here also God leads us into the unknown. We can only follow his promises and walk as children in a darkness, at the end of which an unknown light will shine.

When Consul St. brings us back on board, something happens which—I believe—can only happen to me. I am really convinced, without being able to prove it, that every person has his own style of fate, a sort of "gravitation of reference" which over and over again causes similar combinations of circumstances to come into being. I am always experiencing crazy complications such as I have never observed with any of my friends.

We were dreadfully parched after our visit to the White Fathers and were groaning for something cold to drink or a large serving of ice cream. However, the consul had to hurry to a dinner with some prominent people and insisted upon leaving. He feared that his wife would certainly be nervous because he had remained away so long. So we decided to wait until we got on board for our refreshment. When we got there, we persuaded the consul at least to stop long enough for a cold drink. He then made off immediately but came back crestfallen a few minutes later; he couldn't go on land because our ship had suddenly put off without warning. It had to be turned in order to take oil aboard; and that would require approximately an hour. During this time the telephone connection was also interrupted so that no one, even his wife, was able to learn where the consul was. To whom else would something so exceptional happen?

Safari adventure in the Gorongosa Preserve

Beira
December 10

While we were anchored in Beira I really had no desire to drive through another game preserve. I thought I was somewhat overstuffed with impressions, that there was not much else new for us to see. Above all, I was discouraged by the great heat. We had just experienced a temperature of 41° C. in the shade. If it continued this way the candles would bend during our Christmas celebration on board. But having been so cordially invited and told of the abundance of elephants, buffalos, lions, and even of leopards in the Gorongosa Preserve, L. and I found our curiosity awakened and we accepted gratefully. Since we are both very sociable creatures and regretted having the large car all to ourselves, we also invited along, besides the captain, the chief engineer and his wife and their eleven-year-old Sprat. In addition, our fellow passenger, Mr. S., from Hamburg joined us. Later it turned out that our disinclination to travel alone perhaps saved us. If we had been alone in the situation into which we got ourselves on this drive, it could have been a very serious matter.

When we were awakened at 3:30 in the morning, the steward had already prepared the customary opulent breakfast in the salon. He gave us, besides, some small coolers packed with bread and fruit juices for the journey since we had a several hour drive on the large road leading out of the city to Rhodesia. We enjoyed the relative coolness before sunrise and then turned into an area with narrow, unpaved roads.

On entering the park we were greeted especially cheerfully and eyed with great curiosity. Because of heavy rainfalls, the game preserve had recently been closed. The roads had become too soft, and being stuck in the mud is not without peril. Many parks, especially in the southwest, are therefore completely closed during the summer rainy season. We were probably among the first to come after the reopening. Indeed, during the entire day we met no other cars. Our plans were noted at the toll gate so that a search party could be sent out if we stayed past our planned return. If we had known—but we didn't—that they would set out immediately after 3:00 P.M. when we failed to appear it would have been a comfort during the events we were to experience.

We then saw, as never before, an abundance of wild game: wart hogs, gnus, and entire herds of hippopotamuses. On land they appear in their great massiveness to be figures from the nether regions. Suddenly our driver put on the brakes and turned off the motor. We thought we could hear the earth trembling. A pervasive rumbling roar surrounded us. Then an endless herd of buffalo stormed before us over the road. The columns of dust blotted out the sunlight so that our photos showed scarcely anything. At first we attempted to count; however, we had to give that up and agreed upon the estimate that it must have been at least five hundred animals. From my youth I seem to remember that Karl May once depicted such a storm of buffalos enveloped in dust. Now we had seen something like that with our own eyes.

We could not drive into the area where most of the lions and leopards live. The rainfall had made the countryside a fathomless bog. Where we now were these beasts of prey were seen less often. We would have liked very much to get out, but we had to respect the strict prohibition against it. In the game preserves we had visited earlier not even the roof and windows of the auto were permitted open. The baboons, which like to tumble around and on top of cars, catch hold with their teeth and claws, and that can be dangerous, and not only for women who wear wigs. (We did not run *this* particular risk!) Thus we eyed somewhat suspiciously the trees above us in which the apes were playing. The warning not to leave the car was given us with great emphasis and illustrated accordingly. Only a short while ago in this park two men had been killed: one had been torn to pieces by a leopard after his car had broken down. A gameskeeper who was looking for a missing visitor and had left his land rover was attacked by a lion. Only his shoes were found. An elephant had attacked a Volkswagen, the inhabitants of which finally jumped out in a panic. That was lucky for them, for the elephant contented himself with merely flattening out the Volkswagen. Fortunately we found out much of this only afterwards when we were telling our adventure after our safe return, and the gruesome possibilities to which we had been exposed were described to us.

The roads in the game preserves were still somewhat boggy from the rainfalls, but we were able for the most part to drive around the swampy areas, often through high grass and low bushes. Sometimes the driver roared into a slough with great daring, and after fearful sliding and often also after a near halt the plucky car again gained firm ground.

Suddenly we found ourselves before a giant bog which seemed

to extend endlessly to the right and left. We called to our driver to stop but he had already accelerated to the fullest. It was evident to me in a flash that this power method must fail, and indeed now we were stuck in the middle and things looked quite bad. We were at least fifteen kilometers from the park boundary. The car stood in the blazing sun without any protection. Aside from the fact that we had to try to do something about our situation as quickly as possible, no human could have held out in this burning heat. Even the two ladies and the girl got out of the car. In the shadow of a nearby bush, where it was scarcely less blazing hot, we tried to survey the situation and the possible ways out. It seemed almost impossible to me, but only afterwards did we admit our doubts to one another.

Meanwhile the driver had already begun to break off branches and to lay them under the wheels. He seemed to me to be working in fearful haste. His first attempt to drive out failed completely. The wheels dug themselves in deeper. The tire tracks had meanwhile completely disappeared under the slippery slush which stank of decay. The effect was similar to what we know in our northern winters when a slick layer of snow allows the wheels to turn more and more freely.

Now we began to consider where we should direct the car *if* we should be able to move it. Next to the marshy road we discovered a somewhat firmer place. That had to be our first goal. The captain warned us not to take off our shoes when we went into the hot slush. Snakes and even thorns could be dangerous and we could really not use any new complication. My tennis shoes were soon so black that I could have worn them to a funeral.

At first we carried, in the sweat of our brows (but not *only* of our brows!), sticks and palm leaves from the surrounding area in order to give the lifting jack a firm foundation. This led to repeated failures because the swampy ground always gave way. In seeking in the underbrush for new branches we always had to keep in mind the danger of snakes. The driver admitted to our questioning that he did not have a snake serum in his auto medical kit. Indeed he had nothing at all: no mats, no sand, no shovel, no machete. He said apologetically and somewhat anxiously that he had never experienced anything like this on all his safaris. So we laboriously cut off the branches with a small pocket knife. When we had finally created a complicated foundation under the wheels and Mr. S. turned on the motor, the slick wheels went through and slid to the side, back into the muck, although we tried with all our strength to hold the car from the back and to move it.

We had similar lack of success in further efforts. Meanwhile we had become completely exhausted and we were covered from top to bottom with the disgusting muck, but we didn't show our increasing worry to one another. When I sought to wash off my hands a little in a puddle I could scarcely immerse my fingers, so hot was the water.

Our women conducted themselves ideally, although one could tell how they felt. They kept watch on a herd of elephants rather far in the distance, and combed the landscape with their eyes for other threats. Also, they had searched out a bare tree in the vicinity to which they intended for us to flee if matters got more serious.

My greatest concern was that one of us might suffer a stroke from the heat and effort. What would happen then? Where could we lay him? I thought above all of the captain, who was exerting himself murderously, who would not step into the shade for a moment, and who several times laid his hand on his heart. I felt that he suffered especially and that he was troubled by a sense of responsibility which was certainly not his to bear. But he was accustomed from his duties on the ship to care for the security of his people. Physical effort was not the only message to be read on his distressed features. The least concerned was our little "Sprat." Surely not yet conscious of the danger, she was enjoying the adventure and was amused by the sweat-dripping men whose brows she touchingly dried with their handkerchiefs. Then we sacrificed all these cloths and laid them under the wheels.

Suddenly, one of the women remembered that we still had cool bottles of mineral water and orange juice. In feverish haste they were unpacked. But we had no openers. After a short moment of helpless panic we got a pair of pliers out of the car. Now a small difference of opinion arose among us which showed how differently we reacted to the situation. I proposed to open just one bottle and to have each person take only a couple of swallows. Certainly we did not know whether we would be able to get out at all or when a search party would find us here. So I was for rationing in order that our provisions would at least last until the next day. Our engineer, however, was of another opinion and won out. He said, "What we have, we have. If we drink now we can work better and we'll get out sooner." We were inconceivably parched and poured down all we had.

Since our situation seemed rather hopeless to me, I considered the idea of one of us making our way back to the lodge with the driver, who knew the area, to get help, while the others continued to try to get the car free.

As it later became clear to me, the captain was completely right in objecting to this course, saying that it was much too dangerous, that it would not work because of the heat alone, and that, besides this, the native driver would never agree to it. He continued that we had to do everything that we could to get the car free and, failing that, simply wait for help. When dusk came, he continued, and it got cooler, it would be impossible to walk because the jungle then really came alive. I thought of the passage from the Psalms: "When it becomes night the wild beasts move about." But I pushed aside this recollection. In this case, the words of the Bible were scarcely a comfort.

After this short council, we went to work again. Our two sailors were superior to the rest of us in their sureness of grasp and the energy of their efforts, although we were not lazy either.

After endless, constantly renewed attempts, the car moved a little, then more, and finally we had it—hurrah—on dry ground.

But we still had to tow it through the bushes until we got it back onto the road. That we ultimately succeeded in doing after renewed efforts. We happily got in and thought, Now all the dangers are behind us. To be sure, every swampy place that we had to go past made us hold our breaths. But everything went all right.

Suddenly, we drove directly into an elephant herd which was loitering on the left and the right with its young, and some of which were crossing the road before us. We couldn't go back any more. With obvious nervousness the driver watched for the moment when the road was clear so that he could swiftly race through. That also succeeded in spite of another dangerous-looking puddle. When the herd was behind us, the engineer called to the driver to drive slowly. He wanted to film a magnificent bull which was standing to the side. He would really have preferred to have turned off the motor, although that was not advisable in the proximity of the elephants, and our car was rather sluggish in starting.

But then the woman cried, horrified: "Let's go—they're behind us!" An elephant cow, believing that her calf was in danger, was thundering down on us at full speed. She flapped her gigantic ears and trumpeted loudly. It was a terrifying sight. The driver accelerated as much as possible, and luckily we did not get stuck in a soft spot this time. Finally, we began to increase our distance and got away.

That was the last scare on this safari. We had been awaited anxiously at the gamekeeper's house, and after a short while a search party was sent out for us. Our struggle with the morass and heat had occupied two and a half hours. When we reached the lodge we stripped off our filthy wet clothing and drenched ourselves with wonderful cool water in the showers. It was refreshment without equal, only halfway matched by repeated servings of iced orange juice.

Mercifully, we had been brought safely through all dangers and all difficulties.

This afternoon we are to continue. We are looking forward to the three days of ocean travel to Dar es Salaam after this hot harbor. We are traveling to the politically completely different world of the former German East Africa and present Tanzania— a compound of Tanganyika and Zanzibar. Many tons of copper bars have been loaded on, covered with hides which stink horribly in the sun. I feel sorry for the laborers who must load everything here without fork-lifts. To move the heavy balls of hide, they give forth, instead of the heave-ho so common among us, with a rhythmical sing-song which is interrupted again and again by collective moans and groans. It is scarcely believable that the Africans, even in this backbreaking work, do not sacrifice their cheerfulness. They still have extra energy reserves. To be sure, some of them stretch out exhausted in sleep during the breaks. Most of them, however, immediately begin a chattering palaver. Often only one is the speaker, and now I see one who is obviously narrating something.

But what sort of "narration" is this! While he speaks he makes lively and plastic gestures, jumps about, stoops and stretches himself, and presents the action of a drama. Those who sit and stand about act right along with him, accompanying the show with interpolated cries and roaring laughter to fire the entertainer on to ever more emotional performance. Even the burden and the odor of the hides don't seem to make much difference to them. One of them has cut some cowtails off the hides and twirls them in the air above and behind him, gyrating like a dervish, while the others clap rhythm and accompany the revelry with cries and convulsions. That brings the cowtail dancer to more and more wild ecstasies and causes the clappers finally to join in the dance themselves. A short, wild ballet ensues in the brooding heat of the bottom of the ship as we watch from above, amused but even more astounded. Soon the crane drops down a new load of hides and the spell is broken. Now they moan and groan again as they shift the heavy loads and arrange them upon and next to one another. But even this moaning echoes the rhythm of the dance. One could almost envy these natural men, although one immediately recoils from the snobbism of the thought. But they serve to call attention to the ambiguity of progress and to disturb the naïveté of a blind faith in it. If one drives through their villages and marketplaces one sees them standing together in groups chattering and laughing in front of the huts or in the miserable shops everywhere. They don't seem to know that boredom which is the sickness of civilization. They communicate constantly in group life and a never-failing interchange. If one of them should be seen leaning against a hut, gazing out emptily, that is probably not boredom in our sense. He has simply turned himself off for the moment and entered into the nirvana of complete relaxation.

Much of that which culture has given us beyond these things and has presented us in the way of fulfilled moments, it takes away from us again in another way. The conquest of primitiveness as symbolized in the refinements of life does not always make us happier. When we are no longer disciplined by the whips of poverty and oppression, other rods come to threaten us. And boredom and distress with life are certainly not the least harmful of these. In the welfare states the incidence of suicide rises rapidly—specifically among the young—and drugs are a means to escape the wasteland of a perfectly civilized life. If one walks in Hamburg on the Jungfernstieg or rides on the subway, one does not see as many cheerful and relaxed faces as in the African harbors and miserable villages. On the contrary, the sullenness and emptiness of the average physiognomy there can make one depressed. Has progress really made us happier?

But the question so asked is certainly misleading. We should not criticize progress because it does not seem to hold what we expected. Our misery springs from the growing discrepancy between the outer and the inner condition: between the perfection of the standard of living as well as of the social relationships on the one hand, and the inner hollowness, the metaphysical emptiness, on the other hand. I think of Albert Einstein's perceptive words: "We live in a time of perfected means and confused goals."

Yesterday evening we were still guests in the house of the young couple, v. d. V., in a small neat city castle which belongs to a Belgian company and is furnished with beautiful old pieces. The marble and granite floors in the portico emit a pleasant coolness. That here seven servants are employed, of which some serve the table in a silent, almost spectral manner, impresses us Europeans as an unreal fairy tale. The beautiful swimming pool, in which we frolic before the meal, scarcely cools us at all with its sun-heated water. The refreshing feeling only begins afterwards when we expose our damp bodies to the breeze. Our hosts who, so to speak, themselves live as guests in this representative house, know how to fill the rooms and the hours with dignity and comfort: two young people with style and culture and, at the same time, great cordiality. They might be the hereditary masters of a castle. And of all things, they speak—as scarcely any white person whom we have met before—with warmth and sympathy of their black servants and employees, telling of their touching signs of loyalty and their tirelessness. Only on the farms of the southwest, where the patriarchal, old-fashioned ties still hold sway—ties, by the way, which not only bind the dependents but also the masters—have I met something like this.

Indian Ocean

A day of writing and reading. Again and again we observe, at intervals, hordes of birds which collect at one spot: in the water and above the water a great hunt is in progress. Gigantic swarms of small fish are hunted by large ones. Whoever escapes his stronger comrades and, in flight, gets too near the surface, is in danger of being caught by the beaks of the feathered predators. A hunt and be hunted, an eat and be eaten: this is the nature we appreciate so romantically. And that which we enjoy in idyllic excursions to the forest, gilded by the sun, is at the same time a battlefield. Often the thought of the terror of animals makes me shudder. But no matter how frightening it certainly is, it still does not have the depth and dimension of human fear. The fear of the animal is limited. It remains bounded by the moment in which the jaws of the pursuer gape before or behind it. The animal lives only in the now of an immediate presence, and even in its nest-building or its gathering of provisions there is not a precaution which constantly looks ahead, but rather merely a following of the gift of instinct which limits its impulses to the present moment. Man, however, anticipates the future in fear and hope. The grey ladies of care accompany him and he drags the burden of the past about with him. Man's fear stretches beyond the moment of threat and extends over the entire horizon of his existence. Even Job's or Luther's fear of God had something to do with this anxiety to which the totality of our existence is subject.

Yesterday when we left the harbor of Beira, one of those burlesques occurred which—compared to European relationships—had a very improbable effect. I stood at the exit of the bridge. We had just gotten the harbor behind us when the pilot excitedly sprang to his radio, jerked the antennas out and hurled a torrent of Portuguese into it, which was then answered from the other side just as violently. This was repeated a few times, during which time he had the motors slowed to the lowest number of revolutions per minute. Even the captain didn't seem to be able to make anything out of this chatter, but smiled somewhat sadly when I asked him. He was rather prepared for some sort of strange Portuguese specialty. When we had almost stopped, we saw a tugboat coming up at great speed behind us. The radio girl standing next to me thought she understood from the chattering of the pilot that someone had forgotten something important which was to be brought to us, perhaps a passport or money. When the boat finally reached us—the people of the *Tanganyika* had meanwhile pressed curiously against the railing—a dark Portuguese clattered to the highest level of the bridge, was stopped by someone else with dramatic gestures, and handed one of our sailors a packet wrapped in newspaper. Then the tugboat steamed off again and our machine also left at full speed.

We were bursting with curiosity about what this packet might contain. Finally we learned that our Norwegian stewardess had left her romantic novel back at the port! That had put one of her countrymen (who undoubtedly had good contacts on the tugboat) into such a fit of concern and zeal that he had staged this entire complicated maneuver. The captain said smilingly that things like this were done gladly by the Portuguese. It gave them a chance to perform and put on a show. To stop a great ship, to race behind it with foaming waves, to have all eyes upon them, and at the same time be conscious that they were doing a good

113

deed—that was really something for them. When one thinks how much it usually costs to get a tugboat . . .

We were all bewildered and touched, and at bottom we were glad in our otherwise so rational world to see this arabesque of nice nonsense embroidered. I also thought it nice that the captain did not set himself upon a high bureaucratic horse but took everything with humor. That is typical of him. He is serious with everyone, and laughs with everyone without being anxious about his authority. He doesn't drop another word about the intermezzo with the romantic novel, but just grins to himself.

In the evening on deck mountains of clouds tower on the horizon, filled out in sharp contour by the moonlight. They are of every type between translucent brightness and raven-black darkness. Surrounded by veils of clouds, the white of the stars still shines through them. Astern in the distance are flashes of lightning and ahead of us are the lights of the city of Mozambique and the signal blinker of the lighthouse.

Gradually the mutual reserve is lessening and I am making somewhat more contact with the crew. So this evening I disregard my concern that I could be a damper on them and sit down with a group which is in visible and audible good spirits. Together we sit for a good hour, merry and uninhibited. Then when I go to the lower deck one of them follows me. He steps up next to me, and just as I do, props his elbows on the railing. "I would like to ask you something," he says. "I have no peace with myself. Why am I here? What does all this mean? Most of all, I would like to jump over here; then everything would be over." I am quite amazed. He is a young man with an open, clear face, and I have often observed how he concentrates at his work. He is one of the pillars of the crew. Recently one of his comrades pointed to him and told me, "You can always depend upon him."

And now these words! "What is the matter?" I ask him. "Why have you so fallen out with God, with yourself, and with the world?"

"I have nobody in the world," he says. "That's why I have

gone to sea. At least here one has comrades. I don't start things with anyone; I can get along with them. But you can't tell other people that you have no peace. It is all crap." He uses this word often, and each time he apologizes touchingly, as if he has become too personal with me. "In the ports one has girls, but that is also crap. With them one has only— You understand! And if one should have a good friend—but one can't even talk to him about peace—he is already gone the next time; he has already gotten his discharge. Again crap. But you're a priest or something. Perhaps you can give me a tip about what I should do." Because I really feel sorry for the poor fellow, it worries me that I cannot speak seriously with him in his befogged condition. Every time I begin, he blurts out something else. He is in no condition to listen. The lowering of inhibitions by alcohol is good only insofar that it releases what has been dammed up and allows it to escape in stammered scraps of words. But I ask him anyway: "Have you never known a person who meant something to you or seen a film which gave you something?" (I am trying to understand him further in the hope that we can start from there in a later discussion.)

"Ah, yes," he says. "One person gave me something. Abbe Wotke (at least that is what the name sounded like) with his songs. I have his records and play them again and again." And then he tries to recite some lyrics to me in which he has seen himself reflected and perceived something which helped him along. But he can't get the lines straight, has to start over repeatedly, and then finally breaks off in vexation. I simply cannot succeed this evening in saying something of help to him, although we continue to talk for a long time. This oppresses me. At least I obtain the promise from him that we will continue to talk about it tomorrow when he is himself again. I tell him how much it helps me to read something at the beginning of the day, something which gives me something for the following hours as his Abbe has done for him. He nods but is already far away. Then he goes back to the symposium of his comrades. I watch as he sings with outstretched arms and is toasted laughingly by the others. If I'm not mistaken, it must be one of his Abbe's songs.

A later entry: We never had a subsequent conversation. He obviously avoided me, and when we met, he greeted me in a friendly manner, then pointedly returned to his work. He was embarrassed because he had revealed his heart to strange eyes, although he thirsted to have someone with whom that could be possible. One sees this same old inadequacy again and again on voyages: if the sailors are sober—but not only *they!*—they don't talk about things like that. If they are under the influence of alcohol, the inhibitions fall away, and then the things which they have not come to terms with burst forth from them. But that is not the time when things can be cleared up in speaking and response. Later, however, in the sober light of day, shame again covers the open wounds. I am repeatedly oppressed then by my failure, but I don't know what I should do. At least, I think of them.

At sea
Third Sunday in Advent
December 13

A hot day on a glassy, windless sea. In the morning I spoke upon request in the circle of the officers and the ladies concerning the question of the meaning of life. There is receptive attention and open discussion afterwards. A sailor tells me the crew is indignant that they were not invited. It was a mistake, to be sure, that I only thought of those with whom I normally spend my time. I was glad my friends and acquaintances wanted something concrete to ponder. Now it turns out—and I should not have been guilty of this incorrect evaluation!—that the corresponding need among the sailors is much greater than I assumed. Naturally I am happy about it and tell the man that the Christmas service will certainly offer an opportunity to assemble the entire ship's family for a Christmas devotional.

Tanzania

In Dar es Salaam

Yesterday at supper the captain said: "Just watch—tomorrow morning when we come around the corner, we will see all the ships lying at anchor which were not able to get into port. The time of the simple regulation of traffic is now past. Things don't operate well in Dar es Salaam." We have just now actually entered the waiting room and lie at anchor. Around us at anchor are nine other ships—several English, one Dutch, a Red Chinese, and two Japanese—which are all ahead of us in line. Already rumors are spreading on board that we will have Christmas out here. The old hands try to outdo one another in horror stories about waiting times weeks long that they have had to experience here. Neither do we seem to have an agent who troubles himself about us. In this land of Tanzania, which has been represented to me as Maoistic, all the spheres of ocean travel at any rate are nationalized. There is even talk of an enclave of Far Eastern Communism. I wonder if it is so. This is no private business in the hands of whites, interested in us and representing our concerns. "Here all organization ceases," says one of the officers. I wonder if that is a serious answer to my question as to what the Africans can bring about on their own, and how things turn out when the possibility of free development is offered to them? No matter what experiences the following days or weeks will bring, I must be on guard against an all-too-quick judgment. Something which doesn't function properly could be the manifestation of a sort of childhood illness in this infant country and would therefore be no dependable starting point for prognoses. But I will keep my eyes open.

In spite of these somewhat dark prospects, I enjoy the panorama around me: on the one side a giant dune, upon which is built the lighthouse, grows forth out of the steep coral mountains which are overgrown with trees and which become islands at flood tide. On the other side the city is spread out. We see the steeples of the Catholic cathedral and of the German Lutheran church, the gigantic residential palace (in the German period it was the residence of the governor), the great Hotel Kilimanjaro, and on the heights, sparkling in the morning sun like a castle of the Grail, the giant complex of the new university. The green forest landscape which saturates the view of the city seems on the other side to continue into infinity. The eye lingers longingly on the great, inviting beach. All this lies so closely before us it seems that we can touch it, and yet we have been cut off from it. It seems as if there is no way to bridge the gulf.

The country of Tanganyika, after which our ship was named, no longer exists, since in 1964 President Nyerere convinced the revolutionary council to unite Tanganyika with the island of Zanzibar which lies directly before it, thereby forming the country of Tanzania. A few years later (1967), by the "Arusha Declaration" of Nyerere, all the foreign banks and insurance companies, as well as the economic, industrial, and commercial concerns, were nationalized. The first impression we get of this system is not exactly inviting. But again I say to myself that this is, after all, only the "first" impression.

It is probably the inactivity of waiting which leads my thoughts to turn back again and again to our "jungle experience." One is accustomed, in such moments of peril, to send an emergency prayer for self-preservation to heaven although in doing this, one feels more moved by those for whom one has responsibility than by his own fate. How we were tortured during the air raids with thoughts about the children upon our laps or in the nearby crib! Good—we were preserved and brought through that. But why are there these situations of danger at all—not to speak of those which are without a way out, such as earthquakes, airplane catastrophes, and starvation, which plunge people into a horrible death? Why does God permit the situation at all of having to rescue and then be thanked for it instead of constructing the world system differently and not allowing such occasions to arise? Why, indeed, is there suffering in the world?

When I read the book of Job—and that is what I am doing here, not only for the sake of the meaning, but also to enjoy the fascinating vision of the natural forces—I learn that suffering means education and development. And Augustine speaks of suffering as an oil press: "You will be pressed out. If you are the foam of the oil then you will flow into the drain. If you are oil then you will remain in the oil vat. . . . This pressing out goes forward in the world: by starvation, war, poverty, rising prices, distress, debt, theft, avarice. These are the hardships of the poor and the trials of nations. . . . The scum of the oil is black because it is tainted with blasphemy; it does not glisten. The oil, however, has a sheen. Thus does a man find himself in the same press and in the pressure which grinds him down. Was it not then the pressure which makes him gleam so?"

But I wonder if that is really the solution? Why, then, this whole business with the oil press? Why have we been driven out of paradise to live in a world which presents an insoluble puzzle? I understand dimly the thoughtfulness of the idea that man has frivolously cast away the harmony of paradise, and that as master and representative of the cosmos he has also involved the world in his fate and made it a "fallen world." But did not divine omnipotence have at its disposal other possibilities which could set the world aright after such a convulsion? Isn't this question a variety of the other which asks why the business of Golgotha was needed to bring about salvation?

These are the questions which can never be solved, but which nevertheless must be asked. These things have been for decades and the biblical, theological, philosophical literature is well enough known to permit a survey of the difficulty with which the patriarchs, prophets, thinkers, and poets have struggled in this question. For me the least convincing are all those who try to provide slick solutions through metaphysical baubles. I am impressed only by those who leave the enigma of the fall of man and Golgotha alone in their incomprehensibility and whose faith is satisfied by a grace which, although it can be approached by our thoughts, can never be fathomed.

In the afternoon a first dove comes to our lonely ark from land: a boat brings us the mail. The children, the dog, and the house are doing fine. My entire troop writes me happily from the philosopher's tower in Hamburg that they are still going strong. It is only by a feeling of relief now that I realize I have been secretly concerned something could go wrong during my long absence. I understand what it means to the sailors to be separated from their families for months at a time where they hear of the illnesses of those who belong to them or of the difficulties in school of the children without being able to help.

Dar es Salaam
December 15

On this second day of lying at anchor we all get terribly silly. Because nothing at all is happening, and one cannot always simply sleep in this heat, we hatch out all sorts of stupid ideas to play tricks on the others. And again one of the passengers whom I will call Mr. M. is the welcome victim. He is unusually suited to teasing because he almost always falls for hoaxes people play on him. When we recently found him in a deck chair reading the book *How Can I Become Successful?*, he could scarcely save himself from our good advice for furthering his career and for dealing with people effectively. Every day, precisely on schedule, he does his gymnastic exercises. Knowing his concern for the shape of his body, one person seeks to convince him of the failure of his efforts, while the others praise him as an Adonis. He gladly imparts to any ostensible advice-seeker the secrets of his masculine cosmetic: a powder he especially recommends for hot days and a hair grower which he says has preserved the last vestiges of his hairline. We also learn that he has unusually smooth skin, so the steward teases him about his completely unnecessary razor and the fact that he considers it nonsense that a hairy chest is considered a masculine attribute. We all like him very much because he knows how to have fun, is never annoyed, and is himself most amused when he learns that someone has played a joke on him.

In the evening we read aloud the news from the *Hamburg Abendblatt (Hamburg Evening Tribune)*, which comes over the wireless and is punctually placed on our table by the lady radio operator. I persuade this young lady, who is always ready for fun, to include the following imaginary bulletin among the real news for Mr. M. It goes like this:

Attention, sailors!—In order to give publicity to the prestige of sailors and to those who engage in sea travel, the Federation of German Steamers has organized a competition of masculine beauty for the members of these groups. So that those who are now at sea will not be at a disadvantage, a public decision will be made on 27 January 1971 in the Curio House in Hamburg on the basis of photos which have been received. These photos, which are to show the entire person from the back, from the front, and in profile—bathing suit requested!—are to be sharp enough for projection enlargement and will be received by the first officers of the steamer offices. All those employed on sea voyages in all ranks, on water and on land, between twenty and forty years of age are eligible. The final selection will be at the Frankfurt Book Fair in Autumn 1971. The bodily condition should show a degree of training by gymnastic exercise. Extremely athletic musculature, as well as unusual development of the secondary sexual characteristics, particularly of body hair, are not to be considered as ideals of manly beauty. Among the prominent figures on the judges' committee are Mrs. Wilhelmine Luebke, Dr. Helga Stoedter, and Elke Sommer. Entries should be addressed to 'Masculina 71.' "

It was fantastic how the entire group played along with the joke after the bulletin was read. Some were enthusiastic that something was finally being done for sailors and that it was not only the girls who had beauty contests. Others were indignant about the irrelevance of this plan and feared it would adversely affect the enlistment of young sailors. No one, however, attacked the legitimacy of the report itself. At least not out loud. Mr. M. was the only one who neither praised nor criticized but asked to see the sheet of paper in order to go through the exact wording once again. And when everyone then told him it was his chance to become successful and to rise from the ranks of the anonymous, he was ready to have his pictures made. Only in the later evening, when the matter started to get serious, did we notice a slight change in his attitude. He declared himself somewhat all too strongly to be ready. We had meanwhile taken up the matter a little too enthusiastically, and he had noticed something. Now he was pulling our leg. And for a while he did it successfully.

Before Dar es Salaam
December 16

This morning at seven o'clock we entered the harbor. Luckily the rumors about having to wait for weeks were false. We experienced the picturesque entry from the radio deck. From a distance it is reminiscent—although much more modest—of the entrance of Hong Kong: here too are the many islands and on the shores armies of natives who are probably gathering this early morning to be taken to their places of work in the harbor. On the beach many people are already playing in the water. Even the

122

sailboats of the fishermen all around awaken memories of the junks of Hong Kong. The dock where we tie up at a buoy scarcely fifty meters from the beach corresponds in size to the Hamburg Alster.

The panorama of the city presses close to the shore on all sides. It has a much more hazy look now than it did from a distance. Mr. J., the first officer and also the oldest on board, tells us how different it looked here after the First World War, how much more beautiful the silhouette of the city was at that time. Now it is dominated by the customary skyscrapers and office buildings in their functional international style. The two church towers, which earlier dominated the scene, lead a perilous existence among the modern giants. Immediately behind the stern of our ship is a beautiful two-story building from the German time with overhanging roof and columns which support shady verandas. The black rafters in the walls are reminiscent of mountain houses, and make me a little homesick. Many of these houses, which earlier determined the face of the city right up to the shore, have been torn down and replaced by vapid rectangles of stone.

Nevertheless, the harbor offers the eye much that is charming: the coming and going on board—we are in contact with land by means of boats—the landing and putting off of the ferry boats; the loading and unloading on the many ships all around which are surrounded by barges; the many small customs, merchant, and service boats which enliven the picture.

Because the harbor is completely overloaded and has far too few barges, we are to lie here at least ten days, probably even more. It is also certain that we will celebrate Christmas here— which is really too bad: on the high sea everything would probably have been better organized and also more intimate.

The chancellor of the embassy greets my wife and me and invites us to the embassy. He pours a great deal of cold water on our travel plans. Our machine chief, Mr. D., had projected an expedition of about five days during the layover in Dar es Salaam. It was supposed to have brought us first by airplane and car to

Arusha, that geographical center of East Africa which lies exactly between Capetown and Cairo. From there it was to take us into the different animal preserves and above all into the Serengeti. We had in the meantime overcome the memory of our "jungle" adventure and were thirsting for new adventures. When we tell the chancellor about it we hear the same thing that we hear a few hours later when we visit the embassy: during the Christmas holidays all hotels and wildlife lodges are booked up. Masses of tourists, not least of all those brought by German travel agencies, would descend like swarms of locusts during this time. My allergy against these forms of tourism begins to become virulent when I hear such reports, and I scarcely still want to do it, even in case we could find accommodations. The idea of coming upon great caravans of cars and here and there also traffic signs in a wilderness which has become like a theater backdrop is thoroughly frightening. But is it really like that? I wonder. Our energetic chief does not accept what the chancellor says and begins to make the necessary inquiries on land.

3:30 in the afternoon

The immigrations officer came later in the afternoon together with the agent of our company. For the first time on this journey we meet officials with black skin. But it is another type of African than we have met up to now: young, intelligent faces, lively in conversation, refined manners, not without cordiality. I thought I noticed a certain inhibition toward the whites, but only occasionally. However, it never approaches servility. We go on land with the captain and perspire a great deal as we walk the short way to the office of the ship line. There we see not a single white in the great office. The little room of the chief secretariat of our African agent is the only air-conditioned room and has large windows overlooking the main office room. In this state-run office a native works with great organizational responsibilities—

he also represents other ship lines—and the captain affirms that he is very efficient and pleasant to deal with. In the long-distance telephone conversations he carries on during our visit he is unconstrained and (in an Anglo-Saxon sense) unaffected. Neither are the corresponding details of courtesy and cheerfulness lacking. This type of the young African generation gives me pause to think. Certainly in all too many specimens it does not exist.

Late in the evening

The sharp change of political landscape has a confusing effect on this first day. Although theoretically I knew something of inner African contrasts, one is incomparably more strongly touched when he hears those who are directly concerned speak and is pulled into the stresses of their problems.

A stirring political conversation

In the afternoon the ambassador gave us a reception in his residence at which, to our joy, the captain also took part. The lively, penetrating and long conversation which held us fascinated, touched many nerve points of the East African situation. Luckily the ambassador had invited experts in the problems of the country in various fields. Unfortunately, representatives of developmental help were missing; they were on Christmas vacation. Because of the delicacy of many of the questions handled in the discussion it seems wise not to identify the speakers individually.

The discussion took fire once again—how could it be otherwise!—on the subject of the Cabora Bassa dam in Mozambique. I have probably not mentioned that the Federal Republic of Germany has also taken part in this greatest construction plan of Africa with many millions of marks in developmental monies. Thus the ambassador and his colleagues are always standing in a crossfire between the official, half-, and nonofficial positions of more conservative groups and the revolutionary freedom fighters, who are confused by the contradictory statements of German politicians and are expecting clarification from the diplomatic representative of our country. This naturally demands too much of him. The presence of a German Democratic Republic General Consulate, too, does not exactly make the situation of our embassy more simple.

As I have already mentioned, the political rage of Tanzania is concentrated upon this dam. The belief is that a consolidation of Portuguese colonial rule is connected with it, and the freedom fighters are agitated to their militant actions on the southern border with the catchword "anticolonialism." From these areas, which have been declared danger zones, the partisans swarm into the northern areas of Mozambique, commit assassinations and attacks, and spread discontent and fear.

One of the circle of speakers told me of conversations he had with revolutionary politicians.* He said to them, "You are crazy if you do not let the Europeans finance this billion-dollar project. Basically, they are building it for *you!* Since the anticolonial trend is unmistakable and also inevitable, you Africans will one day be left to yourselves, one way or another, and then the dam will fall into your laps as a gift from your enemies. I don't understand why you are so excited about it, and why all the money given to you is invested in military operations which, given your weakness, cannot accomplish anything. The money should instead be put into schools, hospitals, and housing projects."

Another adds: "These people grotesquely overestimated their military potential. What did they think they could do with their

* The freedom movement for Mozambique, shortened to *Frelimo* (Frente de Libertacao des Mocambique), maintains an institute in Dar es Salaam.

three battalions! A single well-trained company could, if it were in earnest, march from South Africa to Cairo practically without meeting any resistance."

I let this additional remark alone and asked the speaker what the revolutionaries answered to his plea for the dam. " 'That is counting your eggs before they are hatched,' they said. They said that with my European spectacles I couldn't see things the way they really were."

"And how are things, really, or how are they supposed to be?" I asked.

"They reckon thus: the mass of people in Mozambique is politically indifferent because, measured by African standards, they are not doing too poorly. They can only be brought into a specific movement with a great deal of difficulty (and then only very moderately and partially) if one stirs up anticolonial emotions. That is a provocative phrase to which all Africans show definite reaction. If then the dam leads to a gigantic industrial boom—and that is inevitable—they will soon be so fattened by the raising of their standard of living that the last revolutionary sparks will die out."

I express my opinion that the same old conflict is being repeated here: if one seeks to raise the standard of living by developmental helps anywhere, immediately there are people who denounce it as service to the status quo. It was the same way with aid to Biafra: every child whom one saved from starvation by sending aid, so it was said, prolonged the hopeless resistance and continued an undesirable system which was doomed to downfall anyway. If one continues to think in this direction, one is forced to give up all humanitarian activity and is only able then to act within the framework of certain ideological schemata. As far as we Christians are concerned (and I believed this afterwards just as I did before) the basic form of love is improvised sympathy as it was practiced by the Good Samaritan. However, as such a Samaritan, one cannot make his activity dependent upon whether it is helping friends or enemies. One cannot question the status of relationships or correlations to systems. In this world of ours where one constantly thinks in terms of lines of warfare and suprapersonal ethics, it is absolutely necessary to let these signs of direct brotherhood shine forth.

The role of the church in the freedom movement

At this point in the discussion, it was inevitable that I should be asked—as I have been repeatedly before—about the financial help which the Ecumenical Council in Geneva and after it also individual German churches are giving the freedom fighters in Tanzania. The questioner enunciated the principle that one should *not* always play the stopgap Samaritan role in the name of Christian ethics and thereby stabilize the existing rule, but must attack the root of all the evil, colonial rule and racism. The freedom fighters of Tanzania, he said, who operated along this line were thus doing a service to Christian love even if they themselves were not Christians. Therefore they deserve the support of the church.

The man who said this was himself probably not of the opinion he presented. He obviously simply wanted to provoke me, and he had success at that. What the Ecumenical Council has done there, in fact, enrages me. Thus I state expressly my conviction that the church as an institution must never identify itself with a particular group, either of a given political system or revolutionary movement. I establish the distinction between the individual Christian who engages in political activity before God and who can also make forceful political decisions—as I myself probably would if I lived in South America—and the church as an institution which must be independent and for all people. As an official of the church, I am also responsible for the soul of my political opponent. As such I am not responsible for converting him from a direction which I consider to be politically false. The church indeed cannot have the function of a political party. It can only be my duty and task to speak unmistakably and clearly to him about the injustice he commits, according to my opinion, in his political line: for example, allowing inhumane contrasts of rich and poor, perhaps through the political system which he represents; using terror and torture—and much else.

The gentleman sitting next to me at the table, who obviously is especially interested theologically, objects: "But the church can only demand belief if it is credible itself. Doesn't the church become unworthy of credibility, however, when it does not clearly and unequivocally take a stand against an unjust regime—be it a colonial one, as in Portuguese East Africa; or a racist one, as in the South; or against an exploitive dictatorship as in South America? How, then, can it do anything *else* than at the same time take up the cause of the opposition or of revolutionary resistance? Can a simple person handle at all the subtle distinction made by you between the church as an institution and the individual Christian? If he can't—and in this country the people are really *very* simple! —then he will see a church which does not openly condemn an exploitive system radically only as an ideological support of that system. Therefore he will become skeptical toward it."

A delicate theological question

The question in debate here is thereby touched in its basic depth. I am somewhat embarrassed at falling into the professorial vice of lecturing while I am answering it. But everybody encourages me and says that now the subject is broached we must stick to it. I find myself in the remarkable position of a man who has expatiated long and deeply in his written works concerning this question, and who now must say in a few minutes something which requires a long exposition of great complexity. I feel myself strongly burdened by the fragmentary nature of my reply. as I try to make an answer in two stages:

"In the first place, the church itself, as an institution, can never be the bearer of a revolution, and it makes no difference whether this means a bloodless revolution or one by force."

"Well, then, why not?" interpolates my neighbor.

"Well, for the very reason that that group or those persons morally and politically legitimized for a revolution already potentially form the authority they plan to take over. If they do not have this potential, then the alternative to the rulership just overturned is not a new and more just regime, but rather chaos. Thus, merely opposing and criticizing and finding fault in a government does not quite have the effect of inciting or performing revolutionary activity. But it is quite destructive (and neither do I accept the windy argument for the 'dialectics of the negative'). In this course there exists no capability to take up the responsibilities of the regime one wishes to end."

"That's all very fine and illuminating," interrupts my neighbor again, "but I still don't see what that means for the role of the church."

"The significance results from the simple fact that the church as an institution is simply not an identity which takes up or takes over in the sense of a political regime or of a new 'authority.' For, if it were something like that, you could say that it would be capable of the duty of supporting a state. But in what direction would we go if it imagined itself legitimized for such a task? Then Christianity, which is represented by the church, would degenerate to a mere ideology which supported the state. The New Testament as a political credo—would not that be a degeneration? I have already talked too long. Otherwise I could still say something about the separation of the 'two kingdoms'—of the state and of the church; of the world, and of the kingdom of God—upon which separation Luther, as is well known, placed such great value."

After a rather short transitional phase in which we discussed the pros and cons of this doctrine of Luther, and I had the opportunity to emphasize and explain why I supported it only critically and with some deviation, someone said: "You were intending, weren't you, to name yet a *second* reason why the church might not make itself the supporter of political resistance and the representative of a revolution?"

"I have listened with great interest," I continue, "to what you have said about the threatened loss of credibility of the church. Please believe me when I say that this question worries me very much and also worried me during the Third Reich. At that time we were forced to come to terms with this question not only theoretically. I have those experiences particularly in mind when I say: the church by no means gains in credibility by protesting globally against a certain political system. The confessional church and even its most radical representatives could not consider it its duty in the Third Reich to protest altogether and as a body against National Socialism. For the credibility of the church, I believe, it was quite enough to speak out openly against very special sins of the Third Reich, and to call down the judgment of God upon them: against the murder of Jews and mentally ill people, for example. Who else than the church—or more precisely—who else than the Catholic bishop Count Galen and the Protestant bishop Wurm and some others of their circle took that upon themselves? Don't you think even the 'most simple' people, when they learned this and were not themselves ideologically completely pigheaded, respected this protest? Here the church—at least a part of the church—solidarized with the oppressed and beleaguered, and opposed the measures of the regime. But they didn't do so with revolutionary actions or mottoes. I could give you some illustrations out of the circle of the plotters of 20

July 1944 concerning the difficulty with which the church at that time struggled with its responsibility and the rightness and the manner of its collaboration or noncollaboration. I myself was a little involved in these things. And as regards South America: don't you think it would be more serviceable for the creditability of the church to pillory the social injustices of the country—if at all possible with the aid of acute and concrete instances—and to bring to light the torture of political opponents, than to join in revolutionary movements, and then to be only one of those among the bearers of ideology? My worry is that the Brazilian church, for instance, would always be encouraged to make false decisions under the influence of the modish 'theologians of revolution' because it so strongly lacks this watchdog capability."

Sinister German politics

It is impossible to notate the many turns of this conversation which were often so passionate and lasted for hours. Besides these basic problems, it also touched upon very concrete factors, of which I had not learned through our press (perhaps because of my inattention?). For me as a German it was not without pain when one or another of those present showed me that the position of the Federal Republic in regard to the Cabora Bassa dam complex was quite equivocal, even "schizophrenic." A well-known German politician was even reported to have insisted that the government understand that it now had to continue its support for the sureties undertaken for German firms. If it violated the principle of sureties given completely without any political provisos, it would, he said, lead to incalculable effects in the entire world. What this politician, as well as other official representatives, admitted was that the responsibility for the dam was considered a mortgage of the Federal Republic inherited from the earlier administration and that it was essentially thought to be a mistake. Accordingly, the politician had made no bones about his sympathy with the revolutionary freedom fighters and had held out prospects for them in the form of the Friedrich Ebert Foundation. He had also presented himself on a visit to their headquarters but had met with closed doors there, however. Obviously by this snub they had wanted to give him to understand that they did not intend to involve the uncertainty of German politics in this question.

It is a truly odd situation: in this poor land of Tanzania enormous sums are invested for development. Of the ecclesiastical funds devoted to such purposes in general, a relatively large portion comes here. And this country, a minipower economically and militarily, where the average yearly income is approximately 250 marks (!) per person, uses almost all these funds for military operations against neighboring states, in comparison with which it is an ineffectual dwarf. One of the group remarks, "Tanzania strictly refuses to direct developmental funds to their real and authentic primary goals, although this attitude is covered up in its requests for support to the Ecumenical Council where it maintains the money is used in building hospitals and schools and for the salaries of doctors and teachers. One can simply not believe to what ineffective use the money is put in reality. The world press, however, plays up the idea as a wonderful thing and inspires the belief that effective impulses are sent forth from this land for a new order on the African continent. And naturally, here they are quite happy to see themselves justified in the course they have taken."

Of course, it was also necessary to give credence to other points of view, although in this particular group the most varied opinions were represented. I need scarcely mention that this time I did not carry away the triumphant feeling of having finally gained clarity in the matter. The nearer one comes to things, the more complicated they seem. And I cannot even assert that I have come especially close to matters.

I am, at any rate, very thankful to the ambassador that he has allowed me to be present at this play of opinion and to measure the force field of the emerging theses and antitheses in which we are just now moving. Africa is now close to us and yet very far away.

While we spoke together we looked out from the terrace of the residence upon the Indian Ocean. As we were departing, the ambassador picked an orchid for L.

Grand safari to Arusha and the Serengeti

Ngorongoro Wildlife Lodge
December 17

How good it is that the Chief did not lose courage! With the help of a safari agency he has been able without trouble to reserve hotel rooms, a driver and a car. And so we left, in fact, this morning at four o'clock. The boat which was to take us, and whose reliability we were concerned about, was actually on hand. But then began the typical East African complications as soon as we arrived at the airport of Dar es Salaam: instead of the lady radio operator, who had been held up at the last minute, Mr. L. came, our beaming, youthful second officer. For his wife, who, along with the Chief's family, was originally a part of our little safari group, this was a great pleasure. At the somewhat provincial small airport the African functionaries were very meticulous. Although the number of persons shown on our group airplane ticket had not changed, there was now, instead of a woman, a man present. Our Chief, who during the entire trip had been so full of good ideas and had organized so well, was here unsuccessful in convincing the gentlemen behind the counter of the irrelevance of this change. They were devoted to super correctness, and we had to buy new tickets under the pressure of a great loss of time. We hoped later to be able to recover the considerable amount of money involved. This insistence on precise adherence to the rules, which is used in Europe in strikes to slow down traffic, naturally has another significance here. As a first groping imitation of the European style of doing things, it probably represents for these people the epitome of order and civilization. That they have in this so little independence and slavishly hold to the letter of the law is a manifestation of the initial defects of those who have only recently become free. They are still in the stage more or less of mechanical copying. Even if this situation is annoying, I must nevertheless smile to myself because I was struck by a similar example of this attitude in Durban: when our good David was driving us through the Hluhluwe Preserve, he would use the turn signal in the middle of the most lonely wilderness each time he made a right or left, even when he was only driving around a large puddle.

We are glad again to be flying in a small propeller machine. It gives us a completely different contact with the clouds, with the land, and with the water under us than do the giant jets which take one up into abstract heights. This is more like a journey in a stagecoach, as the bumping and being tossed around remind us. One can imagine a wheel breaking as in Goethe's time. We are flying through storm and rain fronts. The sculpture of the cloud formations, which always stands out markedly in this country in contours of light and shade, is in gigantic proportions today in our view from our sky coach. Dark canyons of mist in front of us and behind us, mountains of clouds towering up in the sunlight, ever-new dimensions of an imaginary landscape built on many levels, one on top of the other, have the charm of a splendid fantasy. They are probably unreal because here the formative power does not come—as with geological formations —from underneath out of the earth but creates these airy forms

above, below and from all sides. I am reminded of the words of
the 104th Psalm: "O Lord my God . . . who makest the clouds
thy chariot, who ridest on the wings of the wind, who makest
the winds thy messengers, fire and flame thy ministers. Thou
didst set the earth on its foundations, so that it should never be
shaken."

After a temporary landing at the idyllic miniature airport of
Tanga, we see in the distance, covered with snow and majestic—
like a victory of the earth over all competitive cloud forms—the
gigantic peak of Kilimanjaro. In its middle heights it has collected
around itself a thick wreath of cloud servants which it magnificently oversees. Its cloud-veiled top is seldom seen from below,
but we see it splendidly glistening in the sunlight.

After a long flight over desolate and arid steppes, which from
above would look like a desert if it were not for the occasional
stands of low trees, we land in Arusha. This city, charming and
full of contrasts, impresses us as a half-civilized island in the middle of a truly wild Africa. There are shopping streets in the European style. We even see a fashion shop which looks metropolitan,
has tasteful show window decorations, and is completely free of
kitsch. The white proprietress watches us expectantly and then
somewhat disappointedly as we pass by. We also stroll through
small streets such as we have already seen in the little marketplaces: open boutiques, tailors, and cobblers with their workshops
upon the street. And past all this wanders an enormous mixture
of peoples and races: Indian women in their colorful gowns; men
whose ear lobes have been distended with holes the size of a
silver dollar in which are affixed wooden plugs or long earrings;
ragged, barefooted shepherds who have blown into the city from
the steppes; proud Massais with necklaces, painted faces and
spears; the miserable figures of blind beggars—who can count the
nations, who can name their names! And on the backs of the
mothers, or holding their hands, or running behind them, and
playing everywhere in groups, are children, children. Before one
house lies a large pile of live chickens which are tied together at

the legs—what would our Humane Society say about this? The sons and daughters of the jungles are silent and serious in front of the show windows with the glistening radio sets, cameras, refrigerators, and clothing of the white people. I would very much like to know what they are thinking. This world may seem just as strange and perhaps as frightening to them as their primitive village or their tattered clothing is to us . . .

The driver who, with his safari bus which opens at the top, stands at our disposal for the five-day drive is called Rashidi and is a Moslem. He will become a good and faithful comrade to us on this drive. He is not only fairly considerate and thoughtful of our welfare but also has a genuine passion for the hunt and a curiosity about the wilderness. He is anything but the routine tour guide who only fulfills the minimum. Toward me, the "Professor"— he likes to use this title frequently—he seems at first to have a comical respect. But that is increasingly replaced by surprise that such people as I are not so omniscient as he obviously believed. At first he thought I was merely playing stupid, even when I was, in fact, stupid and did not know about the simplest things which to him were routine. But he continues to handle me with especial care and each time when he hits a hole in the road he turns around and says: "Sorry, Professor!" He probably considers a man of my profession to be especially fragile.

The road to our first destination, Lake Manyara, leads through the broad plains of the endlessly extending Massai Steppe. Again and again we meet the towering warrior figures of this proud race with their herds. Only seldom do they vouchsafe us a glance. In the game preserve itself we can drive closer to the elephants this time, even when they have young. Rashidi is especially experienced; he observes the wind direction and takes care that the elephants do not become disturbed by our scent. He tells us that we can also approach the hippopotamuses closely, except that we must not get between them and the water. Then they feel threatened and become aggressive. With the large elephant herds it is touching to see how the older animals form a protective ring around their young as we cautiously approach. But they remain calm and give no trumpet signals. In spite of our earlier exciting experience with elephants, we now have a remarkable feeling of safety. Rashidi's experience and his sense for the mood of the animals has a calming effect. I notice how, during his drives which often lead far away from all roads over the steppes and through clearings in the bush, he occasionally turns off the motor so that we can observe quietly. This, however, often brings somewhat more risky situations, and he always has an eye on a way of escape. For the most part, we see wild animals in rich abundance and our airy observation post on the roof gives us the possibility of seeing well and precisely. But in spite of all searching, Rashidi does not succeed in showing us the lions which are lurking in the trees and to which this preserve owes its fame.

On the beach of Lake Manyara, where a fresh breeze blows and a few trees give modest shade, we enjoy our picnic and drive in the late afternoon to our night accommodations, the Ngorongoro Wildlife Lodge. It is situated 2500 meters high on the edge of a gigantic crater with a diameter of 15 to 19 kilometers which towers approximately 600 meters above its broad base. Up here it is suddenly very cool. The abrupt change of temperatures is scarcely greater than this abrupt transition from the wilderness to civilization. A fireplace and central heating (during the hot day's journey quite a hellish prospect!) increase the comfort.

The hotel has been fitted into the landscape with taste. Heavy beams and granite are the dominating elements of this architecture. Hordes of servants fill the reception rooms, waiting rooms, and dining rooms. I indulge in my proclivity for a sequestered cultural island in the middle of the untamed wilderness, a proclivity which also determines my love for the ship. The dining room and the guest rooms as well have picture windows which give a view of the giant crater and the peaks in the farthest distance.

The evening soon drops softly down and veils the strange life down below and around us in darkness.

In the morning from out the picture window in our room we see the first elephants down below. On the shore of the lake at the bottom of the crater, broad pink areas are seen, the puzzle of which is only solved by using a spyglass: tens of thousands of flamingoes whose chattering resembles the murmur of a gigantic crowd of people. Before them, clearly recognizable in the telescope, lounge gigantic hippopotamuses. In their great ponderousness and in the winged elegance of the flamingo the entire spectrum of creation seems to be expressed.

But to see all this more precisely we must go down 600 meters deeper to the bottom of the crater. That is only possible with cross-country land rovers or the Japanese land cruisers. These somewhat uncomfortable but stable vehicles are parked in rather large number upon the neighboring plaza. On some of the car doors we even read the names of German travel agencies. Today we will not, as previously, be allowed to be almost alone with the animals.

We travel over steep, narrow roads which are often made of rubble and are full of curves that jar us violently. With two required black "game wardens"—except for wangling tips they are otherwise rather stupid—we finally come down to the bottom of the crater. In this area, which is modest in size in spite of the largeness of the crater, there is an unimaginable abundance of animal life. We are told that in this volcano, which has been extinct now for two million years, live, if it can be imagined, thirty thousand animals—naturally, not counting the monstrous flock of flamingoes! In addition, they are not, as is said to be the case at least in part in many other game preserves, placed here by the hand of man but are the original inhabitants.

The most important thing for us was that we met lions here

139

for the first time. "Tracking" them was not very adventurous, however. One would almost feel as if he were in a zoo if it were not for the strict prohibition not to get out of the car. These giant cats lazily lolling about, seeming to consist solely of indolence and boredom, can gather themselves with amazing suddenness, and our guides repeat the customary horror stories of how the lions have made use of this ability.

We found the lions by the very simple expedient of driving up to a group of safari cars with people on the roofs photographing the animals. What would Winnetou or Old Shatterhand say to this manner of tracking! There lay the yellow beasts of prey in large groups, supposedly camouflaged by high steppe grass. They chastise with a sovereign disdain the staring metal-protected creatures who never shoot at them except with a camera, lifting themselves only now and then to break into an idly supple trot. There was more smell of gasoline than of lions, and again we were moved by the painful sight of tamed ferocity.

It was much more charming to observe a large family of ostriches upon a landscape devoid of people. Father and mother, with dignified step, led their seven little ones, causing our Sprat to exclaim in delight again and again. When we finally drove up too near and Father Ostrich saw his family peace threatened, he readied himself with outspread wings, drawn-up body, and extended neck for an attack upon the offending intruders. Our driver found this so amusing that he drove up to the family from different sides in order to provide us with the spectacle of ever-increasing ostrich anger. I felt almost embarrassed about the brave and so disgracefully deceived bird. The jesting disdain with which we allowed the bitter earnestness of his self-defense to ricochet off us while we sat or stood in a wretchedly secure metal fortress was very small—indeed, quite shabby. Loathesome hyenas sunned themselves before us in the muck. They are, like the jackals and the vultures flying high above us, the garbagemen of the jungle. The thought that they maintain a meaningful and necessary function in nature's household at least makes more bearable how disgusting their business of scavenging is and how repulsive they look. Besides, oddly enough, the hyenas do have some endearing qualities: they are especially concerned for the welfare of their young and for old members of their pack that have become helpless and are no longer able to provide food for themselves. In this respect it is as with men: we also learn to change our minds about another *homo sapiens* who is unfamiliar and unattractive when we see him as the dutiful *pater familias* in his own circle.

The chief attraction of this day, for me, however, was a Massai settlement which lay in a remote spot of the crater game preserve. Only later did we learn that the eighty schillings we had to pay for permission to photograph was the result of a sly deal between our game wardens and the elders of the tribe. That also was a small drop of wormwood in our wish to encounter genuine naturalness. This impression was strengthened by a second when we saw on the shriveled neck of the old wrinkled matriarch squatting in the dust an elegant little key to a safe. Here also the tourist business seemed to flourish and we were not completely without the aids of civilization. But aside from that, the authenticity of what was offered our astounded eyes stood firm: the small round huts made of cow dung were arranged in a large circle and formed a type of community of about ten families. The huts could be connected with one another in the evenings with wooden fences and plaiting so that the great pulpy and trampled area inside the circle was secured against the incursion of beasts of prey. The herds are driven into this area at nightfall.

When we visited the Massais, the spear-bearing men were outside of the village with their herds so that besides the elders we met only women and children. The women, colorful and adorned with many necklaces and pendants, squatted in the grass or on the bare ground in various groups. They plaited mats, sewed, or very simply cared for the hordes of children, one of whom the oldest member of the tribe beat quite mercilessly. The mother seemed to lack the courage to object; at any rate, she watched rather unconcernedly. The almost naked children were pitiable because they were covered all over with flies, but this did not seem to bother them as long as the insects did not get into their eyes. They even let them crawl in and out of their nostrils undisturbed. We were most certainly a welcome change for them, not least of all because of the candy, for which they tirelessly stretched out their little hands. The old ones scarcely noticed us. After so many seasoned tourist attracters among the natives, especially in South Africa, this impressed us as thoroughly pleasant.

As we trudged through the mush into one of these cow-dung villages our curiosity was difficult to maintain against the feeling of disgust at the miserable stench. In the middle were plaited fences for the calves, for which the best place was apparently reserved. The only space left for the people was around the edges. Out of the darkness echoed the whining voice of a baby.

This form of living and existence really lay outside our ability to comprehend. Someone said involuntarily: "And they call this living!" We were, besides, only an hour from our luxury hotel which we could see towering in the distance. It occurred to me to wonder what the effect would be upon these women squatting upon the fly-covered ground if they were to be taken there and shown, for instance, the bathrooms.

This idea reminded me of something I was told about on my first trip to Africa. At that time the Union of South Africa had organized a great industrial exhibit at which there were international examples of the miracles of modern technology. It was probably some psychologists who came upon the idea of testing how primitive bushmen would react if confronted suddenly and without preparation with the instrumentation of technical civilization. Accordingly, ten "wild men" were fetched from the bush; loaded onto a jet plane; flown many miles above the clouds; guided through the exhibition with its agricultural and industrial heavy machinery, kitchen appliances, television, and film showings; and even accommodated in a modern hotel (which brought forth an especially large number of anecdotes about their behavior). Meanwhile, all possible kinds of bets were made concerning what would make the greatest impression upon the bushmen in this strange wonder world. Most bet upon the flight in the Astrojet. But to their very great surprise, a subsequent investigation of the bushmen showed that they completely ignored this experience. Instead, it unanimously affirmed that they had been overwhelmed by something quite different: "These white people only need to make a turn of their hand to cause water to come out of the walls."

I find that this story is very instructive and throws a light upon the processes of understanding: whatever is all too fantastically strange to us we do not truly perceive; it remains unreal because it is without relationship to our familiar life. Thus the jet flight lay beyond the ability of these primitive men to comprehend. But getting water out of the wall—that priceless stuff they so often had to do without and found only with great effort—this had meaning in their own life and impressed them as miraculous. Even miracles, if they are to be understood, cannot be without such association. Perhaps the reports of miracles in the Bible will be put in a new light if one considers that.

When the various safari groups meet later at the small picnic place, we are again in a tourist atmosphere. Even the monkeys up in the trees all around are aware of this. They seem to have a very precise knowledge of the sentimentality of this remarkable creature, man. At any rate, it seems so to me when the mother monkeys make a touching presentation of their young to us and thereby, in spite of the strict prohibition against it, receive many hand-outs. The group of drivers, game wardens, and accompanying police makes camp directly next to us and carries on the customary loud and resoundingly cheerful banter. And then it happens that Mrs. D., the wife of our chief, who is sitting next to me, experiences three shocks, one right after another. While we are chatting and she is taking a bite of a sausage sandwich, a great Indian crane dives down on her, snaps at the bread but instead strikes her finger and beats its wings about her ears. Frightened and in pain, she has scarcely let the bread fall when a monkey springs lightning swift from behind, grabs the sandwich, and then pushes her aside. She brings forth a little scream, jumps up, and in a flood of German sentences tells the dramatic events to the Africans camping next to us. In her excitement she does not notice that these little people understand no German at all. But they perceive from her sweeping sentences that she has something tragic and exciting to tell them and only say sympathetically: "Oh Mama!" For this young, attractive lady, that was the third shock which occurred to her in less than one minute.

When we then break camp in the afternoon to drive into the Serengeti—again with our faithful Rashidi at the wheel—we meet with burning heat and endless steppes and savannas upon which we see herds of gnus, topis, impalas, buffalos, and zebras stretching to the horizon. Completely without pattern, small, steep islands of rock jut out of the even plain—the only signs in the landscape which interrupt the monotony of the broad prairie.

Suddenly, Rashidi, who has been ceaselessly observing to the right and to the left, wheels the car around and races over the steppe and small shrubbery up to one of these rocks. Behind it in the late afternoon sun lies a lion family of four—parents and two young who do not allow themselves to be disturbed by us and who seem to have forgotten that they are dangerous cats of prey. It is unbelievable what the father lion takes from his children and with what patience he allows himself to be teased and tugged by them. Only when it gets a bit too rough does he give them a little slap. Meanwhile the parents groom one another, as if they are petting. It is difficult for us to tear ourselves away from this idyll.

Shortly thereafter we see two ostriches before us, one running before our car and the other one by the side. We decide to determine if they are really as fast as the zoological books say and find

144

that they are indeed. When the speedometer shows 60 or even more kilometers per hour they are able to keep up comfortably, while our car almost has difficulty making it on the bumpy road which is crisscrossed with furrows and tracks. It reminds me of the quotation about the female ostrich from the Book of Job: "God has given her no understanding. But when she is frightened, she puts horse and rider to shame." We also discover two cheetahs, those fastest of all animals that are said to be able to run 90 to 120 kilometers per hour. They are very shy and take to their heels. Our repeated attempts to drive around them and stop them again are not successful.

Finally, after a drive of several hours through the Serengeti—the preserve is almost as large as Northern Ireland!—a mountain appears before us, the ridge of which consists of wildly jutting stone. Here also is situated the Lobo Wildlife Lodge, in which we intend to take up quarters for two days. But it is difficult to make it out with the naked eye. It looks so much like a part of one of these great stones it is scarcely to be distinguished from them. It is as if a creation of the hand of man wanted to be part of nature here and, in common with many animals, has been camouflaged with a protective covering.

When we finally arrive we find a structure of peculiar architecture indeed. Its individual wings, its passages, steps, lower and upper galleries, are fitted into the towering rock. Steps running back and forth lead to a small plateau with a swimming pool from the perimeter of which, where tables and chairs are set up, one can see far across the green forested landscape until the view finds its limit in the distant hills. A mountain stream ceaselessly pours gushing water into the swimming pool. By African standards, it is refreshingly cool. As we quickly plunge in to rid ourselves of dust and perspiration, we notice that the bottom of the swimming pool also consists of natural stone which swiftly falls away from shallow to deep water. The great hall and the dining room both have glass walls and include the cliffs. In part they form the wall, and in part they jut out into the room in bizarre forms. Where there is no natural rock are heavy beams and granite. Here and there among the series of tall, slim wooden pillars which bear the ceiling beams is a living tree, the top of which extends through the roof into the open air. Its trunks are enclosed by glass cases lighted from within. They, along with the long lamps which hang down, are the sources of light for the room. The trees and bushes which grow in the rock gardens and in part grow close to the glass walls are also lighted and thus related to the decor of the dining room. Since the rooms have not been *a priori* designed freely, but conform to the arrangement of the landscape, there are different levels in the large sitting rooms and cozy corners hung over by rock which are further sequestered from one another by amenable lighting. All this increases the intimacy of the individual seating groupings without separating them from the rest of the great room. Thus, from our corner we can observe the scurrying hither and thither of the many waiters and the coming and going of the few guests. Since the hotel is still new and has not even been officially opened, they do not seem to be quite used to strangers. The black youths enjoy talking with us; they are friendly and well-trained and are very interested in where we have been and where we are going.

After a highly refined dinner, we retire to one of the two large fireplaces in which the boy periodically piles up more logs. Enchanted by the abundance of impressions and by the comfort of this novel room, we allow the day to fade away in conversations which evoke renewed memories of the rich hours we have just experienced.

When we retire for the night, the sounds of the wilderness penetrate through the open screen windows to us, a croaking and chirping we scarcely hear any more now that weariness has drawn her veil over us and allows us to sink into a deep, dreamless sleep. Only now and then are we briefly startled by the penetrating laughter of hyenas.

146

This morning, while the others are again on safari, I have stayed behind in the lodge. I need a respite to digest impressions, to make notes, and to read. When I go with paper and writing materials to sit in a quiet place in the sun—here at 1800 meters altitude this is a comfortable possibility—the boys immediately guess my intent and, unrequested, bring me a chair and a comfortable writing desk. The waiters have alert intelligent faces and react with precision and dispatch to all requests thus making a new contribution to my thoughts concerning what can be made of Africans, or what they can make of themselves . . .

While writing I observe again and again several adama lizards which scuttle around on the sun-warmed rock immediately next to me. Several times I have the feeling that they are looking at me to determine whether I am a friendly or hostile creature. The males are splendidly colorful—blue and coral red—while the females are less striking. This does not seem to damage the relationship between the sexes, however.

Every morning upon arising we read a few verses of Christmas carols together. We notice again in doing this how closely Christmas is bound up in our imagination with the winter gloom of our homeland. We find it difficult to awaken what one calls "Christmas spirit" in this early summer atmosphere. For us Christmas is simply connected with snow, twilight, pine trees, the light of Advent, and the aroma of Christmas pastries. But without all these accompanying feelings and moods, the message of the Christmas carol strikes us in all of its immediacy. Scorning all the emotional crutches which frequently do not support, but rather throw up a smoke screen, it invokes the relevance of Christmas. Nourished only by the Word of God and Christmas carols, the message of the "extreme mercy" of God arises in undistorted clarity—like the stars shining above us in the tropical night which no earthly haze causes to pale or flicker.

After we had said good-by to the Lobo Lodge early in the morning—not a very easy thing to do since we had really put down roots there—we were soon driving through the Serengeti again. Vultures circled over us again and again, dropping down in a definite direction, whereupon Rashidi turned off the road and drove cross country. There approximately two hundred meters away, we saw a leopard retreating with a great piece of meat. Immediately to the left a hyena was apparently tearing at a cadaver. As we drove up to the hyena, it ran away and we could then see a freshly torn small antelope, a Topi, lying on the ground. The hind portion has already been dreadfully mangled. When one considers that this tiny, elegant animal only a short while ago had been jumping about, the very picture of life. . . . But this is, to be sure, the sentimentality of a domesticated man of culture who does not think of the illogicality of enjoying wild game at table and then recoiling when he sees the sudden bloody fate of a creature in the natural state. The leopard and the hyena, naturally, see all this in a quite different light. For them the antelope is not a creature which enjoys life, but nothing other than something to eat. Tiger and hyena live in the directness of their instincts. Conflict and contradiction of thought have their genesis with man. His is not a world of unambiguous instincts. He also has the urge to eat and satisfies it by killing, but he also has the faculty—and is at the same time damned by it—of seeing creatures in their suffering. He has the drive to fight and to assert himself. He destroys his enemy, or at least persecutes him with hatred. But he also has the faculty —and is at the same time damned by it—of recognizing the human visage in others and seeing the look of pleading. This, his conflict, is also the hope of humanity. By his command that we love our enemies, Christ has deepened this conflict, prevented us from forgetting it, and simultaneously created something of the highest human value. He has revealed to man his secret for atonement and shown it to him as a promise. Strange what thoughts the dead little antelope, the leopard, and the hyena evoke in me while the car has long since continued its journey on the wide, wide steppe.

Lunch break at Lagaja by Lake Natron. Since its water is unpotable and there are no springs available, water for drinking and washing for the safari camps which have been set up under tents must be brought in by tank truck. During lunch my glance is drawn again and again to the head of this camp, a Hemingway type of imposing form, with a gigantic, elaborately curled moustache. He had earlier been a big game hunter. What stories he must be able to tell!

Toward evening we meet in the Manyara Lodge and view once again the Ngorongoro Crater. The circle of these superabundant safari days is drawing to a close. For the first time we experience a hotel packed full of guests and indeed showing something of the dreaded fullness the German ambassador had predicted. Many different languages babble in the rooms. There is scarcely a skin color that is not represented. We are happy to have caught the last quiet days and to have experienced a wilderness almost free of man.

Dar es Salaam
On board
December 21

This morning on the drive back to Arusha, Rashidi calls our attention to some huts of the "Arusha people" standing alone and very distant from the city. As farmers, they are different from the nomadic Massais, but, like them, live in a primitive manner. Their huts have a simple framework of wood, or, more accurately, of staves. We ask Rashidi to gain us an "audience" with these people, and then follow him at a measured distance so that he can feel them out in advance. He has told us in the beginning that these people are very shy. Indeed, tourists do not come here. Besides, the government forbids these people contact with that species of people—probably for the simple reason that they do not wish the efforts at progress of this country to be held up to cheap and caricaturing ridicule by reports and images from the outside. But it is precisely this which lures us. Here at last one may harbor the expectation of seeing something genuinely original.

The negotiations seem to be difficult as Rashidi speaks to the people animatedly. But the expressions on their faces are veiled. As we finally, however, slowly approach the large family assembled in front of the hut and I somewhat prematurely adjust the light meter of my camera, Rashidi energetically waves a warning to me. The head of the family glares at me angrily and threateningly gesticulates with a sword-like instrument. He had intently been cleaning a primitive plow with this "sword" while Rashidi was speaking with him. When our driver carefully draws out a ten-schilling bill from his pocket, their moods become somewhat milder, and we are allowed to walk about. On the ground squats an ancient grandmother with wrinkled face and head shaved bald, caring for the numerous small children. They are also shaved bald, and some of them wear the customary wooden plugs in their ear lobes, which are enlarged by the great apertures. To the side, surrounded by young women and teenagers, stand two wizened old men of whom I have the impression they are seeking to calm the still excited family. A feeling of discomfort is beginning to creep over me. I feel that here we are crashing in and disturbing the untouched peace of this family. As glances of mistrust are directed again and again upon the camera, which is still out of its case, I lose the desire to torment them with it. The spokesman of the family, an energetic and rather unfriendly middle-aged man, even jumps under the eave and calls mockingly to us—Rashidi translates it—that we can take pictures of his legs. Later, when we have traveled on and are about to take a picture of a picturesque group of women carrying large banana baskets on their heads, they turn away in frightened panic and take flight. I experienced this fear of the camera again and again in East Asia; here I meet it for the first time in Africa. This fear of the magical power which surrounds pictures is like the magic of name in archaic realms: whoever knows a name has power over the bearer of that name. (The name Jahwe, signifying God, is not spoken by the Jews. One would be presuming to gain a blasphemous power over God.) It is precisely so with the picture as with the name: whoever has a picture dominates the one represented there and has him in his power. By making a hole in the picture he can thereby commit the subject of the picture to death. The magic of analogy which binds together form and representation belongs to the powers of magic. Because it would be an unforgivable crudeness to torment these troubled "wild people" further with our presence and the threat which it seems to present, we soon leave there, waving to them in a friendly manner in order to reassure them a little.

In Arusha itself, where we visit our safari office, the worst part of our journey awaits us: for the seven people of our group there are only three seats on the airplane. Even telephoning and negotiating for several hours changes nothing. The situation is quite desperate. Our two sailors must absolutely get back to the ship, and there are neither trains nor buses. To rent a Volkswagen bus as a taxi for a distance of over nine hundred kilometers would be exorbitant, and, in addition, round-trip fare would also have to be paid. There would be no place to stay overnight on the journey, or even a source of food. For the three women and the child that would be quite difficult. In the vague hope that perhaps we could fly from the Moshi airport about thirty kilometers away we race there with Rashidi. Time is extremely short, and it is uncertain whether we will be able to catch the airplane there at all. If it is already gone, or full, we are in a devilish situation. For right now, just before the holidays, everything is booked up for half a week.

We are therefore extremely anxious whether we will be lucky, and Rashidi presses down on the accelerator desperately. In East Africa if the only means of transportation at one's command vanishes, one is really helpless and begins to feel lost and abandoned.

When, with tongues hanging out, we arrive in time at the little airport of Moshi, the Indian manager, with only the first slight hint of a gratuity, places two airplane seats at our disposal. We give them to the second officer and his wife. The manager indicates there is a possibility to receive yet two more seats. If that works out, my wife and I can also go along, and the D. family would then use the three flight tickets we have to make the trip to Dar es Salaam. If that doesn't work out— We don't dare think about it. The manager allows the matter to dangle for a good while, although I suppose he is prepared to manage things in a positive manner. But why does he leave us hanging? Well, that is not hard to guess. When we really come across with the "tip" for his efforts, he tells us beamingly that four hundredweights of meat will be taken off the plane and thereby two more places will be gained for the Thielickes. . . .

Nyerere a Maoist?

In the airplane we are surprised to meet Dr. Walther, the chief physician of the Kilimanjaro Christian Medical Center of Moshi. His work is in many ways related to that of Albert Schweitzer and is somewhat known to me through the biannual circular letters he sends out. We greatly enjoy this unexpected meeting and listen while he tells us of his far-flung work. From his center in Moshi, a great and modern clinic, he manages, with the help of a small airplane, many hospital branches which he has set up and for which he has educated native nurses. When he tells how difficult it is to carry on this educative work with the minimal school requirements here, I ask this experienced man the customary question concerning what he considers to be the possibilities of development of the African people. His answer is similar in many ways to the opinions of Dr. Haape, whom, by the way, he does not know. He, too, attributes the previous historical inferiority of the blacks not to natural temperamental characteristics, but rather the fact that they have lacked natural and historical "demands" and accordingly do not think beyond the moment. "In your journey to Arusha," he says, "you have certainly seen the peculiar bunches of maize the people have hung in the trees. They do that because when they store it on the ground the rats get it. But in the trees the birds get it. Having found no effective means of conservation, they reason then that the best thing is to eat the maize. Afterwards we will eat the bananas, they say. There is always something. Thus they live from moment to moment, and this style of life naturally contains no stimulus for planning and foresight."

Just as the judgments of men whom I consider especially competent are surprisingly similar, the political expressions of Dr. Walther are different from anything which has been said to me concerning the regime in Tanzania. Again I see how confusing the aspects are in which can be seen the same things and how easy, therefore, it is to be made a fool by a one-sided orientation. The measured manner in which Dr. Walther expresses himself, and his personal acquaintance with many leading personalities of the country—his great medical center naturally has caught the attention of the government and his medical position leads to many personal contacts—cause me to consider his opinions especially valid.

He also knows President Nyerere. When I speak of the fact that the president, according to all I have heard, is a very gifted, although a very ambiguous and, with his demagoguery, a very dangerous man, Dr. Walther firmly contradicts me. He affirms that Nyerere has certain demagogical characteristics, but that he holds this under control. His emotions do not run away with him; they are rather based upon a real consciousness of mission. Besides, he is a highly gifted, cultivated, and thoroughly cultured man. He also possesses a complete academic education. He is familiar with European universities.

"In his photos," I reply to Dr. Walther, "which one sees in all hotel lobbies, offices, and stores, he looks rather fanatical and grim. I am struck by his piercing eyes."

"This is an artful public relations photo that does not represent him as he really is," comes the answer. "In personal association he is anything but fanatical and morose. On the contrary, he is easygoing and completely relaxed. Not a trace of the hysteria of Hitler! He is also completely honest, personally modest, cordial, and without any pomposity."

I ask Dr. Walther to tell us still more about him.

"What I find particularly noteworthy," he continues, "is his style of life. He avoids above all any isolation in the higher echelons of the state's hierarchy, seeking contact with the simple people and spending half of his time in the villages. He wears nondescript civilian clothing and drives a land rover. Besides, you would have to look for a long time and perhaps even in vain to find a statesman of his breadth of culture. He has translated Shakespeare into Swahili and is making great efforts to raise that tongue to the level of a cultural language." I learned further that he has established committees of philological specialists which have created a vocabulary of technology and the natural sciences in Swahili and annually publish their lexicographical works. Although at this time English was still the main language of instruction at universities and colleges, Nyerere was working to have it replaced eventually by a highly refined Swahili. Dr.

Walther said it was unbelievable and fascinating to experience what a fullness of sound this African language possessed and to what a polished precision it could be refined when Nyerere used it in one of his great speeches.

"And what about his Maoistic connections?" I asked. "On the ship and on land I have heard again and again that it is the Chinese who are really in control here even if they remain in the background. I believed I was seeing a certain affirmation of this when I observed the preference with which the Red Chinese ships were treated."

Dr. Walther also contradicts me here: "Of course, it is true that Nyerere was strongly impressed with his visit to China and that he borrows much—by no means all!—from there when he considers it suitable and importable. But the rumor that the Chinese have him in tow is, however, either malicious or stupid. Nyerere indeed wants socialism and, for example, considers the Kolchose to be the organizational form suitable for production in his country. This is nevertheless a very serious problem! One must not imagine that our European ideas of democracy can be realized at every level of development and can be imported everywhere."

I assent: "Democracy is the institutional expression of a certain political degree of maturity. If democracy is not synchronized with this stage of maturity and is forced through at the wrong time, it creates only chaos. Democracy as an abstract doctrine out of kilter with history can be frightful."

On the other hand I asked Dr. Walther whether he is not being too optimistic when he refuses to consider the idea that Nyerere is in the Chinese camp. I remind him of the gigantic undertaking of the railroad construction for which the Chinese brought tens of thousands of workers with them and also provided the material. I further mention the industrial undertakings of the Chinese I have already encountered in this country.

"The building of the railroad is a good example," answers Dr. Walther. "Nyerere resisted the invasion of the Chinese worker masses for a long time and at first stopped the project altogether.

Only after the Chinese insisted they would build the railroad solely with their own workers—and besides no other power was prepared to take over this task—did Nyerere relent and let the Chinese in."

"And the revolutionary freedom fighters? The partisans against the Cabora-Bassa dam? This looks a little bit like Maoistic practices to me."

Dr. Walther demurs: "That is a kind of obsession with them. Here they are simply confused." And then he repeats exactly the same argument I already heard in the conversation with the guests of the ambassador. I only mention it here because he also gave a good example: "Let them go ahead and build," Dr. Walther had said to some representatives of the freedom fighters. "You will get the dam in the end anyway. When Mussolini invaded Abyssinia he built streets and airfields there. And yet the Italians cannot use these things any more. Whatever the Abyssinians have of such facilities today they owe solely to the Italians. It will be similar with the dam. Why are you getting so excited? As I said, that is simply an obsession."

In Dar es Salaam we take leave of Dr. Walther. We wish him luck in his negotiations with the government and express the hope that he will be able to accept our invitation to dine on board with us another time.

On the ship the boatswain receives us at the gangway with the report that it has rained heavily here and that the loading had gone much more slowly than had been expected in any case. "We will certainly not get away before the 28th of December and perhaps we will even celebrate New Year's here."

This is a small blow. Can I remain so long away from my work? One of the officers advises me: "Whoever comes to East Africa must adopt another sense of time. The best thing to do is simply to check it in at the door." The more I think about it, the more attractive it seems to me to try to take part in this exercise. I would learn little on this trip if I did not also experience this change in the sense of time. I would seem to myself the very paragon of a "tourist" if I got into a rush even here and allowed the reckoning of my work quota at home to become master over me. So, just let the sabbatical pass away . . .

At noon the ambassador and his wife return our visit to them. There are smoked pork ribs, knockwurst, and kale—a banquet better suited to an icy winter than to the super summer of Dar es Salaam. For this reason the air conditioning is set extremely cold and our guests seem happy suddenly to enjoy selections from the kitchens and cellars of their homeland in this tropical latitude. At any rate, the cheeriness of our conversation rises to a high degree and this time I do not disturb the enlivened diplomat with my probing questions. Immediately afterwards he and his wife set out on their Christmas vacation journey.

Medical care in Tanzania: Help for self-help

Wednesday

How nice that Dr. Walther could accept our invitation for supper. His talks with the authorities have lasted longer than expected and he is still here.

When we afterwards ask him over coffee in the salon to tell us something more of his work here, much concerning the structural situation in this country comes out. It is like the old saying: when one looks at a circumscribed situation "from all sides" he sees the entire matter often more clearly than in the so-called large survey.

Dr. Walther's activity as a missionary-doctor is defined by the immense need for medical aid. While at home a doctor cares for about six hundred people, here it is twenty-five thousand. The will to help of this doctor is not simply expressed by his founding of a hospital, surrounding himself with assistants, nurses, and orderlies, and seeing to the medical needs of those who come to him asking for help. That would be, so to speak, the "old" form, which earlier was the sole manner in which Christian love was practiced, like a medical charity in an emergency case laid before one's feet. I have already written that for us today the parable of the Good Samaritan reveals itself in wider dimensions: we are summoned to a systematically planning providential and preventive love. For the doctor—and especially for the director of a "Christian hospital"—this includes, for example, the duty of changing the conditions under which there is in Tanzania, but probably also in other East African states, such an immense child mortality rate. And here half of all the children die before the fifth year, chiefly on account of an unbalanced diet: Maniok or Kassa root, not unlike our potato in taste, forms the chief means of nourishment for the people, and it can be dangerous for the children who depend solely upon it. The concrete goal of a providential and preventive love must be of a form which facilitates self-help and thereby frees the recipient from dependency upon the benefactor.

It is in this line that Dr. Walther's activity as a missionary-doctor lies as he trains natives as medical assistants. Naturally, this can only be an abbreviated course emphasizing the completely practical. "But they can do a Caesarean and also an appendectomy," says our visitor. "There are also other small operations they do perfectly. And just think what it means in this wilderness when there are people who can do things like this. Besides," he adds, "you would be surprised how accurate they often are in diagnosis. Here, in fact, their instinct is not spoiled by too much education."

In cooperation with these native auxiliary doctors he can maintain six branch hospitals in his district. And since he has over 250 of these men, he has contributed to the fact that there now is a doctor or auxiliary doctor for every 15,000 (and no longer 25,000!) inhabitants. In general, he says, one would not be able to operate without these native helpers because in Tanzania there are 120 tribes with 140 languages. In addition, the gigantic distances can have a devastating effect if there is a scarcity of personnel.

I mention then that I have always been impressed by the fact that Albert Schweitzer in his Lambaréné hospital allowed the family members to stay with the sick, partly to avoid severing them completely from a familiar atmosphere, but also because he used the family members to help in the care and for other services. I had also seen this in a remote country hospital in the Philippines. Did Dr. Walther do this?

"Oh, yes," he answers, "we do that too. These people have such a highly developed sense of family and tribe that their isolation as patients would bring them into a therapeutically unfavorable situation. Besides, we would not be able to take care of our central hospital with its 320 beds if we did not have help from the families."

I ask further: "Out in the country there are probably serious cases in which your auxiliary doctors are helpless. What do they do then? Can they get into contact with you?"

"Yes, they can, and the method is not unlike the way someone on a ship is helped when there is no doctor on board. Our small branches in the country are in contact with us by radio. There is a certain hour of the day set aside for inquiries by our auxiliary doctors. This is, naturally, an enormous psychological help for them. In serious cases, a time is set at a later hour for another contact when the appropriate specialist is made available. In especially complicated situations which the auxiliary doctor cannot handle, our aircraft, donated by the Rotary Club, arrives with doctors and nurses. The pilot, an English student who is at our disposal for two years, particularly enjoys making landings in the wilderness and steppes."

We are especially interested in how Dr. Walther manages to maintain this complicated and extensive operation financially. He reports to us that there are in his area four parochial hospitals, one private, and one state hospital. In the entire country, half of all hospitals are supported by churches and missions. The government pays only ten percent of their expenses. Everything else must be raised by contribution. This is also true with him. In the parochial and mission hospitals treatment is free. It must be paid for in the state hospitals.

"Permit me one more stupid question," I continue. "Do you limit the patients you treat free only to the members of the Christian community?"

Dr. Walther raises his hands in a negative gesture: "On the contrary! Naturally, we treat everyone who comes no matter what his religion."

"But what if he has none?" I ask.

"Naturally we do it then, too. But for Africa that is a rather unrealistic idea. Atheism is found only among some few intellectual Africans who have studied in Peking or in a state of the Eastern bloc. With them we have practically nothing to do."

My question about a possible preferred treatment of Christians causes him to express himself a little bitterly about the often-heard criticism that medical missionary aid is a slyly calculated undertaking to corral sheep for Christianity. In reality it is a selfless ministration (even if Dr. Walther perhaps does not use this somewhat high-flown expression). It must indeed have a very depressing effect upon someone who has dedicated his life to his work in this way when he hears his service called into question by such insinuations. And it is really a matter of sacrifice (this word, too, is not one of Dr. Walther's own expressions). He is a prominent physician who could have gone a much easier and certainly a more profitable way with a German university faculty. And his entire family must also bear the burden of his task. How difficult the education of the children; how early they must leave home! It touches us greatly when he says: "That my children have endured all this without bitterness and without reproach against their parents, that they have never ceased to support my work, is for me the greatest reward."

We are still curious to learn how a modern hospital furnished with all the latest equipment affects primitive people from the bush, for instance, the Massai. "They like very much to be treated by us," Dr. Walther smiled, "but there are often some curious reactions. Recently one of them said to me: 'The last shot which you gave to me did not work. But the one before it, it was good. I can still feel it today.' You must also make medicine taste as bad as possible so that they know it is working."

An interesting formula for health

The word "Massai" cues me to continued questioning: "These people interest us very much. They are proud and imposing figures. Even when alone with their herds on the steppe they are not without their 'masculine cosmetic.' They are carefully painted and their hair is powdered with ochre."

Again Dr. Walther smiles: "They do that in order to keep lice and other insects away. That has nothing to do with the aesthetic intent of make-up." This is quite sobering for our enthusiastic romanticism. He continues: "That these people have made such an impression upon you is typical for tourists. [Of course, we do not enjoy hearing that.] These people are really constitutionally primitive, and I do not believe that they are capable of further development. For foreigners they are quite attractive, with their erect carriage, their size, their ornamentation, and their warlike spears. Among the Africans themselves, however—because of their primitivity—they are rather looked down upon. The fact that they look so healthy in general and have such splendid teeth is based upon their good eating habits, which distinguish them from the others."

We have often asked ourselves what the Massais live on when they are with their herds on the endless steppe far from all settlements. What Dr. Walther then tells us causes us to shudder a little: "Of course, they eat the meat of their herds and also wild game they have killed. Their chief source of nourishment, however, is a curdled mixture of blood and milk which they drink daily by the quart. They obtain the blood by tapping the veins of their cattle and then closing the wounds again. They prepare the mixture of blood and milk very skillfully. They hollow out a calabash—a type of gourd—which they then rinse out with urine and so sterilize it. This blood-milk mixture is very healthy and rich in vitamins—and it doesn't taste so bad, by the way," he adds, grinning.

We endeavor to suppress any grimace of disgust (this would make a bad impression upon a doctor!). I only ask: "Do these people, then, know something about bacteria?"

"Naturally not. But experience has taught them that the milk gets well soured by the treatment with urine and does not solidify. In their own way they have discovered the bactericidal effect of urine."

We ask what sort of sicknesses the natives have most. Among those which he enumerates I remember that in this country there are 150,000 lepers; that is, 1.5 percent of the total population. On the other hand, in fifteen years among the Africans he has as yet encountered not one single heart attack. This cannot have to do with the cholesterol which is customarily made responsible for heart disease in the popular medicine of the press; the cholesterol content of meat is high.

We then express the supposition that these people—for example, the Massais—probably experience fewer pressures. Dr. Walther disputes this. "A lion hunt is quite tense. Tribal and clan feuds are also pretty tough. I see quite a different explanation: illnesses such as heart disease do not originate simply from mere excitement but from the stress of career ambition and unresolved conflicts. People here are spared that more than in Europe or America." When one sees himself as a civilized man in the mirror of so-called primitive life, completely new forms of self-recognition can arise.

In all that was discussed on this evening, I was also impressed by what our visitor told about the poverty of this country. Of the twelve million inhabitants of Tanzania there are only four hundred thousand who receive salaries; that is, people who have some sort of job. That is one-thirtieth of the entire population. Ninety-five percent are farmers who for the most part buy nothing, but only work for their own needs. The economic and social contrasts among the rural population are extremely stark. On the one hand are the poorest devils who wrestle their barest necessity from the stingy ground with antediluvial tools. On the other are the well-to-do coffee farmers whose plantations allow them a splendid style of life. On special occasions these families use their airplanes to visit one another.

What contrasts! What tensions are also here! How poorly one can judge all this by European standards, especially the political attempts to bring this structural confusion under control and to direct its development to desired goals . . . The nearer we come to Africa, the more it exceeds our grasp!

A visit to the University of Dar es Salaam; Positive and negative aspects of developmental help

Dar es Salaam
December 23

We are very fortunate to have spent a large part of the present day with Pastor Jahnel and also to have the prospect of being enriched by being with him in the following days. With his young family he has lived for several years in Dar es Salaam and ministers to the German parish and numerous far-flung native communities. He speaks perfect Swahili. And he has, in addition to his clerical office and in connection with it, concerned himself intensively with the psychology of the natives, their art, their esoteric cults and practices, as well as with the political problems of the country. He is an unbelievably vital, exciting conversationalist in whose company we see more than we have on any other occasion while at the same time receiving the necessary explanations.

Before we drive to the university, which I naturally would like to see, as always we visit the market. It is full of noise and odors and overflowing with people. One booth stands out in my memory above all the rest. Here a man had a large table upon which were one hundred small bottles with liquids of various colors. For the people visiting the market he was no small attraction and was enthusiastically surrounded. We pressed to the front and found a sign with an index of the individual little bottles and the effects which their mysterious liquids were supposed to produce. Pastor J. translates it for us: These are helpful medicines for eyes, ears, teeth, heart, and many other organs, but also occult preparations, as, for instance, one which is recommended for those who want to get ahead in their job and to "gain a promotion." We will have to tell Mr. M., who is reading the book *How Can I Become Successful?*, about this. Only my shyness prevents me from buying this bottle for him.

Even the road to the university, which is situated far out on a mountain, is an object lesson in the circumstances of the country. We see the large complex of buildings of a Chinese textile factory, which, with the building of the railroad, is the greatest developmental undertaking in Tanzania. But the Chinese do not seem to have gone to excessive expense here because the newest looms, as Pastor J. tell us, are from 1909. The Chinese have used machinery here which is obsolete for the industry in their own country.

Shortly thereafter the road leads us past whole colonies of new housing developments. They have been built by the government in a program of governmental housing and have been essentially financed by German developmental aid. My ears prick up: this then is *also* accomplished with developmental funds. Obviously they don't all go into the pockets of the freedom fighters and partisans. Of course, I don't know what ratio of distribution has been used here and what its relation to the prevailing circumstances may be. Nevertheless, one notices how easily a report can be biased. Naturally I am far from making the assumption that after this short trip I shall be in a position to gain a comprehensive and objective view.

Looking over the expansive university campus sprinkled with great modern buildings, we nearly have our breath taken away. We seek to attain an orientation from the roof of one of these skyscrapers. What we see is comparable to the imposing design of the newly constructed Ruhr University of Bochum, yet *here* we are in one of the poorest parts of Africa, in the neighborhood of impoverished huts and cottages! In addition to the institutes for research and teaching, there are a number of magnificent dormitories. Although we cannot tour them, I confidently believe that the living comfort of these quarters could scarcely be less than the splendid design of the façades. And again I ask myself whether students who live in these surroundings for a few years will not be estranged from the milieu of their homes. Will they, as physicians, for instance, want to return to the poverty of the bush and of the villages?

When we tour the campus and buildings my feelings become more and more divided. On the one hand I am happy to read on every building that it owes its existence to a generous contribution from America or one of the European countries. (Here is another case where developmental aid has again *not* found its way into the pockets of the militant revolutionaries!) On the other hand, one is oppressed with the question why everything must be so luxurious. Could not everything have been made more simple and yet functionally sufficient? Could not additional schools and hospitals have been financed with the funds? Does one really believe that he is doing service to the Africans with this nouveau riche island in the middle of an ocean of poverty and primitivity? Did they not simply really want to flatter their vanity and serve their own prestige? I do not believe that these thoughts of ours are motivated by a malicious criticism. The impression comes all too much to the fore that people here want to outdo one another in splendor and luxury. Unfortunately, this impression grows to an absolute certainty when we see the pride of the entire area, the great hall donated by the Federal Republic of Germany with eight million marks. I also thought until now that our new Auditorium Maximum in Hamburg belonged to the great accomplishments of modern auditorium architecture, and now I see that the great hall of Dar es Salaam is to some degree more impressive. It is covered with an extremely expensive copper roof which we none too parsimonious Hanseatics would never have been able to afford for our purposes, nor even for the much smaller dome of our administration building. (We settled for a painted imitation of verdigris.) Here the floor is inlaid with the finest parquet woods upon which, however, are somewhat shabby plastic chairs. When we express our surprise at this

166

aesthetic barbarism, Pastor J. explains that plastic in this country is a symbol of progressive modernity. Therefore these synthetic products were preferred to more suitable furniture of wood. Well, this may be one of the aesthetic childhood illnesses of awakening nations and is to that extent unimportant. But I can't get over the fact that tax and developmental funds from the Federal Republic are wasted here for mere affectation while no thought is given to real efficacy of its use and, above all, no sensible planning is done. We surprise ourselves suddenly with expressions of outrage, and our displeasure grows even more when we learn that we actually competed with other nations for the right to build this bombastic structure. Finally, it was given to the country which was prepared to construct it in the most luxurious fashion. That was our country.

On the drive back Pastor J. gives us another interesting statistic which is very revealing about the participation of religions in the academic area: in the entire country are 51 percent animists, 21 percent Mohammedans, and 28 percent Christians. Of the students, however, 84 percent are Christians, 14 percent Mohammedans, and 2 percent without religion, that is to say, Maoist atheists who have studied at Eastern bloc universities. The disproportionately high percentage of Christians in the intellectual upper class is the result of the mission schools.

The wood-carving of the Makonde

On the drive we visit various Makonde wood-carving workshops which are set up close to the street. We see the chiseling, hammering, filing, cutting, and polishing of many African artists—and some of them really are artists!—and we are fascinated.

167

Pastor J., who possesses a large collection of these sculptures, discusses with several of the carvers what they think about as they work. This is especially interesting and instructive with the many surrealistic sculptures. Until now I have seen in them only a play with form. Though in this sense I had found them charming and meditative, it is astounding, however, what comes out when one listens to the conversation of the carver of such "abstract" sculpture. In a manner which we are familiar with, for instance, from Picasso, we find the human anatomy torn apart: occasionally a lone stylized ear or an oversized eye emerges. These are symbols that one is being heard and watched over. The waves which are often to be found at the foot of the sculpture signify the underground forces from which threat proceeds. One surrealistic image, which especially pleases me in its play of form and which I purchase, is like a picture puzzle. Only after an explanation by the artist does one learn to see in this intertwining of forms the references to human organs, the arrangement of which remains hidden by bizarre and at the same time distracting swellings, cavities, and ridges. "That is the evil and invisible spirit of the steppe," the man explains to us. He eludes identification; he is everywhere and nowhere. He must be sought for a long time before he is found. The *cantus firmus* which permeates this art is the confessional of fear, the expression of threat from all sides. Here one catches a glimpse of the terrors of an unredeemed world.

The objective representational forms of animals and people are, on the other hand, very much less ambiguous and without horror. In them one can see repeated again and again a column cut all around with reliefs of up to eighty heads. They represent a genealogical tree and the succession of generations: below are the grandparents; above them the parents, the children, the children's children. It is as if here the individuality of the single member is set aside and the security and tradition of tribe glorified. The temporal and spatial relationships of everyone are, so to speak, the *real* individuality, within which we have only the rank of members. Here man has not yet awakened to what Kierkegaard calls the "individual." This awakening only occurs where man is "called by his own name."

A dark chapter: corruption

In the afternoon we swim in the fine pool of the Hotel Kilimanjaro near our ship. A man seeks to favor us with a red "Mao Bible." I have no wish for it; besides, I have been familiar with it for a long time. Some black mammies who are sitting nearby like watchful shepherdesses are touching and tirelessly caring for their white wards. Now and then there is some sobbing childish distress. But whenever one of the mammies presses her child to her great bosom and surrounds it with soft warmth, everything is again soon all right.

Lying in a deck chair, I get into a conversation with a Tanzanian businessman. When the conversation touches the question of corruption, I recognize in what he tells me a confirmation of something I have already heard from another side and which we ourselves experienced in the little landing field at Moshi. It was extraordinary, he said, how one had to spread bribes everywhere if one wanted to accomplish the most simple things. Even medicines for his wife, pressingly needed and prescribed by the physician, and sent with a great deal of effort from abroad by airmail, were not handed over to him by customs, in spite of all remonstrances, and in spite of the intervention of the clinic. He tells us then of the thieves' cant by the veiled allusions of which one probes an official to learn what amount of bribery money would induce him to change his mind. In spite of his revulsion, he had no other choice in the case of the medicines than to play the game, and so he finally received them.

169

This reminded me of a lecture on a socio-ethical theme which I once gave in Argentina. In the discussion that followed I was asked: "What is the largest bribe a Christian should accept?" The question was not: "Should one do this?" but only: "How large a bribe is one permitted to accept?" Torn between irony and help-lessness I blurted out: "Up to 10 percent . . ." (which of course is a completely impossible utterance from a theologian). I was simply curious as to how the audience would react. I was, so to speak, feeling my oats. Horrifyingly enough, they agreed with my estimation and said, in essence: "Since in this country things cannot be done without bribery, the most important thing is to have *some* limit. One should not be permitted to enrich himself excessively by this means. If one consciously accepts a self-control one shows that he is not without a sense of responsibility." This astonishing reaction gave me pause for thought. Not that I affirm corruption! On the contrary, I would count it one of the most important goals of a statesman to put an end to it. But as long as it *exists*, how are we to deal with it? Didn't we ourselves on our safari make a modest attempt at bribery because no other way was left open for us? I consider it dishonest to set up abstract and radical postulates of Christian ethic when it is clear to every-one that they cannot be followed at all, that they are not followed and that there is no intention to follow them, because, "Things are the way they are." Thus it has subsequently dawned on me (and now again during this conversation at the Kilimanjaro swimming pool) that the limit of 10 percent for corruption was not at all as absurd as it seemed to me at first. Could not—*rebus sic stantibus* [with things remaining thus]—the respect of the "limit" really be the ethically most important thing? And if brib-ery within this limit is a type of prescriptive right: *is* it then actually still corruption? At least, then, it no longer occurs in secret but has the openness of custom to its credit. And it would be related to legal control in its limitation. Perhaps this "strain" of corruption is a type of counterbalance to ponderous, rustily grinding bureaucracies. This would be then, so to speak, a matter of a bureaucracy softened by corruption! One cannot heal the sore of bribery—and naturally it is a sore!—if one does not first bring the organism of bureaucratic structure under control.

I hope no one who reads this thinks I am making a plea for corruption! That would certainly be as unfair as it would be, in my case, dishonest if I were to remain quiet concerning these thoughts which occurred to me. Rather, I am moved by the passion to place myself completely within other contexts to accomplish a change of norms and to prevent my standards from petrifying in a doctrinaire fashion. Sometimes this doesn't work, of course, as perhaps even here in this matter of corruption. But I would rather risk a fiasco than to retreat back to the stage of smugly assured criteria. I detest the defeatism of the "orthodoxy" which fortifies itself in the closet of seemingly unshakable but unrealistic formulas. I am proud of the freedom of a Christian who may dare heresy to gain the truth. The freedom to which the gospel calls us also includes the freedom of bold and venturesome thought. God will not despair of us when we err.

I have become hot in the deck chair—not only because of the temperature but also because of this hot subject. So I plunge again into the water and enjoy the bliss of creaturely pleasure. Even problems cannot always be cracked. Occasionally they must simply be drowned. I believe that is a law of creation which has survived the Fall.

Organizational childhood diseases

In the late afternoon while writing in my diary, I look up again and again to watch the heavy copper bars being loaded. Completely rusted tugboats bring the material to just as shabby barges.

I am amazed how skillfully a convoy of several of these heavy boats is towed to the side of our ship. But that is the only thing there is to admire here. In contrast to South Africa and Portuguese East Africa, I see the predicted disorganization actually confirmed: if the material is brought in the barges, then the workers aren't there; another time it's the other way around. We are struck also by the laziness and clumsiness of the dock workers (even if one does not use the loading virtuosos of Hamburg or Antwerp as a standard). Only a fourth of them work, and even those with a minimum of effort. The other three-fourths have gone to sleep or are chatting or giving the workers advice. This division of labor, which obviously has been agreed upon, actually works! The bars, which are stacked one on top of the other, constantly get scrambled. Looking down from above one gets nervous for he can see the mistakes the men are making in loading and what must happen in the next moment. (But I wonder if the advice I could give would be better than that given below?) It seems to take forever until they have the scattered cargo together again. The loading officer is in despair: "They simply cannot load with neatness and order!" Soon I find myself again believing the theory that they have no perception for the geometry of the right angle! Our sailors express their rage vehemently. Socialism does not show its most attractive side here. "It's just that competition is lacking," says one sailor. "Private firms give promotion on another basis. There must be some interest shown, otherwise everything goes wrong, especially if the organization is fouled up. And here again this results from a lack of interest." The economy of the free market and competition, with all of the questionable things associated with it and with all its possibilities of degeneration, have nevertheless one decisive plus: it puts the essential drives of human nature, namely, egoism and interest, into the motors of the economic processes. Egoism in man apparently must always undergo a certain transformation if it is to be creative rather than destructive. Either it must be sublimated or used as an impelling force. In its raw state it leads to excess, to the struggle of all against all, or, on the other hand, to sloth and indolence.

We also become annoyed at the many times when the boat which is to bring us from the ship to land comes too late or not at all. Pastor J. explains to us that in Swahili there is no expression for "to be late" but only the passive form "I was detained." Whether that makes one feel himself to be the victim of unfortunate circumstances or of evil spirits is not known. In any case, however, one is a "victim" and requires no excuse. In school that could drive one mad. There are things which one as a European can simply never get used to.

The trauma of the black man

Midnight

In the small apartment of the pastor where the captain, the first officer, and we two spent the evening and enjoyed cordial hospitality there was already a Christmas tree, a sisal bush beautifully decorated with fruits from home. Thankfully, it was not like the Christmas kitsch which so painfully attacks us in shops and hotels. We admire the selected display of African sculpture which J. and his wife, who is a connoisseur and shares his work and hobby with him, have brought together. The conversation once again takes up the subject of the constantly repeated fear motif. Animal symbols for hostile powers are the serpent and, above all, the chameleon. "Why, of all things, the chameleon?" we ask, whereupon our host tells us a Tanzanian legend which touches us greatly and almost shocks us. "Originally all men were black. In this ancient time God gave heraldic animals to each of the continents: Europe received the gazelle, India the elephant, and Africa the chameleon. One day God summoned these heraldic animals to give them a message for their continents. When they had assembled before his throne he gave them their commission. 'Hasten back to your lands as quickly as you can,' he commanded them, 'and tell the people there that they are to bathe in a lake. When they again climb out of the water they will no longer be black but white.' The heraldic animals did as they were commanded. Naturally the gazelle was the fastest and delivered his message first. Thus the Europeans bathed first in the lake and immediately their skin became white. The elephant was very much slower: however, he delivered his message next. By the time the Indians went into the lake the Europeans had polluted and discolored the water with their once black skin, so it was no longer able to wash the Indians completely white. So they became brown, the color of earth. The chameleon required the longest amount of time to return to Africa. When the Africans finally came to the lake, the water had dried out and become a shallow puddle, and it was no longer possible to submerge in it. So in their despair they put their hands in the shallow puddle. And thus it is that they are the only ones who have remained black and only the palms of their hands are light. Since then the chameleon is the most hated of animals. It has become the embodiment of the evil powers to which all misfortune is owed."

How shocking is the accusation that speaks from this etiological legend—not only the reproof for the chameleon and basically for divine providence which ordained it as the heraldic animal, but "between the lines" also for the Europeans who undeservedly "always get there first"! Also moving is the deep inferiority feeling expressed here.

While we sit on the parsonage terrace by the Indian Ocean and the storm lanterns flicker softly in the breeze, we speak further concerning the relationship of white and black as it is expressed in this story. "We no longer can go back to the Southwest," say our hosts spontaneously and simultaneously. "It would be impossible to serve in the framework of apartheid. Here we are in uninhibited and fraternal contact with one another. Here our message does not suffer from unbelievability because Christian solidarity suddenly stops at the racial boundary. We visit our African friends and parishioners in their houses, have meals with them, and are cordially received without any reserve."

"Do you also receive them here at your house? Do you often sit so comfortably with them on your terrace as this evening with us?"

"Naturally," answers Mrs. J. "I have the impression that they are comfortable here and feel completely at their ease. Only with the women do we sometimes have difficulty. They often beg off at the last moment. But if they do not come, as a rule it is because they cannot conquer their self-consciousness. This probably has its basis in the inferior position of the woman. It will be a long time yet until that is overcome."

As if in illustration of this, a couple is announced, the husband a black. The wife is from Munich. He, too, speaks pure Munich German. They had gotten acquainted there. When they become aware of our presence they immediately start to leave, but as good friends they are welcomed and brought into our company. He is a journalist, well-educated, cosmopolitan, charming, and skilled in conversation. It is as if the charm of his Munich dialect is enhanced by the mildly guttural sound of his voice. In spite of all the sympathy one involuntarily feels toward the two, there is still a sense of discomfort and strangeness in regard to this union. Is this the voice of my instinct? Or is this the effect of prejudice? Still perhaps it is not the bias one owes to his upbringing: the pastor later tells us as he drives us to the harbor that he, as a minister, has had many sad experiences with such mixed marriages. When the period of sexual excitement is past, a difference becomes notable as a rule, which causes suffering and estrangement for the couple as they get older.

At the harbor the boat which was ordered is naturally again not there. Finally with some effort we succeed in finding a taxi boat to our ship.

Christmas Eve in the church at Dar es Salaam and on board ship

On deck, ten o'clock in the morning: melancholy mood on the ship. At breakfast there was scarcely a word spoken. Everyone thinks of home. The D. family has been very upset by a telegram. The accommodations for the children will have to be changed. The mother is to come home immediately. We advise and console. The matter can only be cleared up by a telephone call to Hamburg. The helplessness at this distance is really great. And this of all times at Christmas!

This afternoon we are to have a small ship's party with the crew. The captain has become monosyllabic. He is probably brooding over what he is to say. Since we are all going to hold a Christmas Mass afterwards which I will conduct, we agreed that this time he would not read the Christmas story as usual.

I sit in the glimmering heat on deck in a shady spot and think about what I am to say. Most importantly how shall I give the message of Christmas to the young sailors so that they are touched by the peace and joy of this night? There is a thick layer of melancholy camouflaged with joviality and sarcasm which must be broken through. Only the spirit which is able "of these stones to raise up children" and which has nothing to do with human—all-too-human—ideas can break through these walls. That does not preclude that I make a very great effort and seek especially apt examples. I will write it all down and think about it thoroughly.

About midnight

Now we have behind us the first Christmas Eve we have spent on a ship.

As is customary in South and East Africa the church was decorated with a disturbing carnival appearance: garish garlands, paper bells, and similar kitsch which does not make it exactly easy to create the right spirit. Pastor J., with his aesthetic sensibility, last Christmas was no longer able to bear this cheapness, and with his wife he decorated the church in festive but more subdued dignity. "The congregation reacted quite bitterly," he says, somewhat embarrassed to show me the paper streamers waving in the wind. "They felt themselves cheated of the familiar festive joys, and they mutinied. I finally saw my reformer's zeal as an aesthetic phariseeism—there is such a thing, right?—and said to myself: there are 'weak brothers' in the realm of taste also whom one should not annoy. Let them have their fun, too." This thought helped me to overcome my repulsion.

The walls of the great church, which is located on a lively street, are punctured with holes and slits for air circulation. Nevertheless everyone was bathed in perspiration. The openness of the church permitted all the noise of the traffic to penetrate within besides. I had to use all the strength of my voice to be heard. This vocal labor in combination with the white liturgical robes insured that I left a small puddle of perspiration on the floor of the podium. The worst thing, however, was that I could see neither my notes nor the congregation. The late afternoon sun was shining directly through the open portal into my face. It not only increased my temperature, but made me totally blind. I had a small moment of fright to overcome until I could forget about what I had prepared and launch out into the open sea. I had to trust that, in the wind which swelled my sails, there was also a breeze from the Holy Spirit. In any case, I experienced the joy of bringing the gospel. Even if I could not see the congregation, I felt the supporting power of a mass audience. The Christmas songs also aided mightily in bringing the message, so that we returned to our boat satisfied and happy in the mild evening and were taken back to the ship.

There, by the way, the short celebration that had been planned in advance had already taken place. When the captain began to lead "Silent Night, Holy Night," a few eyes became moist—the young fathers and mothers had their melancholy thoughts—but others, especially the young, were terribly embarrassed and sought to conquer this feeling with self-conscious grins.

That evening, when we sat with the crew in the officers' mess, made a strong impression upon me. The young officers, not wanting to leave any of the sailors, stokers, and ship's boys to their helpless loneliness, invited them to their rooms for abundant hospitality. Even though the majority had gone on shore, a considerable group was brought together. After some Christmas songs, things became merry and loud, but no one "fell out of character." Someone said to me touchingly: "It probably seems odd to you that we are observing Christmas so loudly. We are only doing this so we won't hear anything moralistic." I well understood that. There are indeed none too many who are touched by the essence of the Christmas message. The person who lives on mere Christmas "spirit"—on the fragrance of the Christmas tree, the intimacy of the family circle, the warm nest of home—feels himself quite abandoned here in the far reaches of the tropics. And yet, in spite of all attempts to hide feelings behind noise and beat music, there was a last evidence of the radiance of the Christmas message: it was clear the officers were not only officers but men who wanted to help to fulfill this evening—or perhaps to conquer it. The idea would never occur to consider this the result of Christmas love. And I too in my conversations have diligently avoided this term. Nevertheless it was imprinted upon my mind that even the hardest, most reserved men and even the shyest boys went out of their way to come up to anyone on deck, press his hand and wish him a "Merry Christmas." It is remarkable how everything is thawed and melted by the warmth of this season—even at such great distance from the source of this warmth. It would be snobbish to dismiss all this with the pejorative term "sentimentality."

Later we went with the captain, our esteemed and provident

steward, and our small safari group to the comfortable living room of our chief, D. There we spent a long while in good conversation. As in the mess hall and in the salon, so here also was a genuine Christmas tree which had been carefully preserved in the cold storage compartment. We were suddenly transported to a Christmas at home. The air conditioning completed the illusion. When later we shall have returned again to our northern land, our pleasure will be scarcely greater than our surprise at this imaginary home atmosphere.

An overland journey at Christmastime: Encounter with the mission

Dar es Salaam
Evening, December 25

I sit on deck writing. The lights of the city and of the ships lying about are reflected in the water. The light wind which causes ripples and gives movement to the reflections fans a refreshing coolness. It is very still and I think of Job's "songs of praise in the night."

On this first day of Christmas we accompany Pastor J. to a Christmas service at one of the villages in his parish. When we get into the car, a great, festively clothed throng is streaming into the Catholic cathedral near the harbor shore. Pastor J. visits several of the villages in his parish every Sunday to hold services, to baptize (about 40 to 50 children monthly!) and to offer spiritual advice. His diocese, comprised of over twenty congregations, is half the size of Bavaria. He must cover approximately 800 kilometers on the three Christmas days this year. Since the services last two to three hours, and many visits must yet be made, this, considering the long, hot, dusty and bumpy road he must travel at the wheel, is an almost unimaginable effort. That he does it cheerfully, in a relaxed and seemingly tireless way, is probably due not only to his robust constitution but also to the joy which enlivens all his ministrations.

In this manner we came to the completely isolated native village of Kisarawe. Since strangers scarcely ever come here, our appearance—especially on Christmas morning—excites no small amount of attention. The drive over the lonely bush roads and through the extensive palm forest was adventuresome and rather like the exercise one gets on a morning's horseback ride.

Since we arrived in plenty of time, we rested in a small over-grown cemetery containing eleven graves of early missionaries and their families. Here also rests the first and most important missionary, Greiner (1842–1905), who worked for almost twenty years in the Dar es Salaam area. While we stood in this great loneliness between the graves, Pastor J. was able to tell us so vividly of the lives of those resting here that we actually seemed to feel their presence. These first missionaries made sacrifices which our pampered generation can scarcely appreciate. Many were taken by malaria or blackwater fever, so that Bodelschingh once called his people back home. He had the impression, not without reason, that the Europeans could not exist here at the current level of tropical medicine in those days, and that the dying of his missionaries and their families in such great numbers was unjustifiable. His decision led to a falling out with Greiner, who, in spite of everything, intended to continue his work rather than abandon the newly formed congregations. Since he now was thrown back upon his own resources, he established for self-support a plantation which brought him great success —he was an amazingly efficient and indomitable man. The millet seed he brought from Germany flourished so surprisingly here that a neighboring tribe asked him to bring them "another seed" which would create the life of which he spoke in his sermons—an arabesque on the margins of the Christianization which is instructive and not without some humor.

There was scarcely a missionary in whose family the tropical illnesses had not produced a fatality. One of them had to send his wife back to Europe because she could not bear the climate and remained separated from her for ten years. As a rule, families were separated: the children were educated in Germany and often returned later to the mission field to continue the work of their fathers. In this hot and malaria-poisoned region they held out—without automobiles, without air conditioning, even without housing in the case of the first ones (it had to be built first), without the knowledge of the language—lonely and cut off in a strange world. As we were told all this in the small cemetery I remembered the biography of Traugott Hahn. His father spent eighteen years in the bush separated from his children before he baptized his first convert—eighteen years!

While I stand before these graves, it seems silly and even mad that certain people say missionaries were the beadles and vanguard of colonialism. It is not customary to have this degree of dedication for such goals. And when one thinks of the accompanying circumstances and the by-products of missionary work, the first thought that comes to mind should be, rather than colonialism, liberation from the dreadful bondage of magic—only a simple salon romantic lacking both in knowledge and imagination could lament that! One should think of the establishment of schools and education, of auxiliary doctors and nurses, of the humanization and culture which the work of these pioneers accomplished. The present-day science of mission work operates with incomparably more subtle methods of religious knowledge—I have already mentioned this. It makes use of the sciences of sociology, psychology, and anthropology; it also recognizes that the great missionary pioneers were sometimes clumsy and misinformed. And yet we are touched in this cemetery with a feeling of respect for the dedication and the sacrifice of these forebears. It remains to be seen whether we, with all our cleverness, will attain a fraction of this dedication.

The conversation then came around to black and white magic

which haunts not only the animistic areas but is also here under the cover of Christianity. Black magic is destructive and brings ruin to men and beasts. White magic is constructive and healing. There is an antidote for every form of hex and destruction, so that the harmony of all forces of life can be restored again. Pastor J. tells us some quite horrible events—from this very congregation—which we would scarcely credit if he himself had not been involved as a witness and had not been required to come to terms with them in difficult conflicts.

The name of the parish in which we are then driving is translated "Height of Hope." Here Greiner settled freed slaves whom no one else wanted. It was difficult when a former slave girl wanted to marry. Marriage agreements were made between clans. The husband's clan had to pay a sum for the bride. It remained untouched and was at the disposal of the wife if the husband died or divorced her. The emancipated girls, however, had no clan to represent them. However, Greiner worked out a plan: he simply adopted them, and it is highly amusing to hear still today that various old Negro women and men who have the name Greiner live here. Of course, there has been no lack of evil tongues that have attempted to interpret this relationship of names in another way. But this is, in fact, slander.

Christmas service in the native village of Kisarawe

For the first time in our African excursions we have the impression of being in a place which could be called a "picturesque little village." The small houses are scattered about under the palms, sparkling clean and well taken care of, truly an unusual sight in these zones. Next to the little church the bell is hung on beams. The children ring the bell and take great pleasure competing with one another to grab the cord. Then the congregation streams in from all sides, and soon the church is full to the bursting point. We sit closely hemmed in and perspire while we sing in Swahili—even without a knowledge of the language one can pronounce it easily—the Christmas carol, "Lo How a Rose E'er Blooming." Not without a secret pleasure, I tell myself, "Now we are coming to the lines '. . . in the middle of the cold winter, deep in the night.'"

The service, with the Lord's Supper and baptism, lasts two whole hours, but as far as we are concerned it is too short. The longer it lasts, the more powerful, violent, and full-voiced does the Christmas singing become. Especially passionate is the participation in the more rhythmic of the songs of Anglo-Saxon origin. There do not yet seem to be any original native songs. During the sermon which we, of course, do not understand, I leaf through the hymnal. It is only with difficulty that I suppress a grin when I come upon melodies such as "I Have Devoted Myself" and "A Call Booms Out Like Thunder." But whatever may seem liturgically questionable melts away when one hears this collective devotion and spirited Christmas singing. If there is an aesthetic phariseeism there is also certainly a liturgical one!

The charming little candidate for baptism cries pitifully when the pastor sprinkles him with water. During the final part of the first liturgy the large mammy undoes her obviously newly purchased city dress with the help of someone behind her and quiets the child at her breast. Soon it is full and asleep, and the mammy turns to the other children around her to rock and cuddle them.

We all take bread and wine then and with the song "O Blessed One" go outside in front of the church where the sunlight sparkles around us and the pastor ends the service. Afterwards there is cordial handshaking on every side. I had said a short word of greeting during the service, and now they know that the white strangers also worship the Child in the manger.

At the very end there is another surprise for the children.

Many little packages of clothing wrapped in newspaper distributed among them. The pastor gathered them as cast articles in the German congregation of Dar es Salaam. When see the radiant eyes of the children I think of the many overfu Christmas plates on the ship which our sailors for the most part left untouched. I chide myself that I did not think of bringing them along for the children. The crumbs from the tables of us who are overfed would have caused a storm of jubilation among them. Another thing about which I cannot think without anger is the expenditure which we make in building our new churches at home. If only we could make them more simple! We would not only become more credible at home but could use the money here for purposes of the gospel instead of squandering it in ostentation and tomfoolery. Here the pastor does not even know how he is going to find bicycles for his preachers and catechists, without which they will not be able to cover the great distances. In a much poorer neighboring community only one member of each family can come to the service because there are not enough clothes to go around and they have to be passed from one person to the other.

When we finally arrive again in Dar es Salaam, exhausted and wrung out, we jump into the water to refresh ourselves. The pastor, however, has no time for that. He quickly gets a bite to eat at home and then immediately starts out again for his next Christmas service in a village which lies much further off. And tomorrow there will be two such journeys upon which, as usual, no one accompanies him. And day after tomorrow the same thing. Everywhere he must present himself fresh and in good spirits. Everyone awaits him with yearning since he comes to them only once in eleven weeks. It is hard to comprehend how he goes at this pace and still keeps his cordiality genuine and without a routine quality. He knows for what and for whom he does all these things. Therefore he can "rise up like an eagle; he can run without becoming tired."

Excursion to Bagamayo, the city of the slaves

Dar es Salaam
December 26

Today we traveled with the captain to Bagamayo across from the island of Zanzibar. The road led for a long way through the sand and the car rolled and skidded and rubbed the bottom between the tracks in the road. This excursion was to be a journey into history. We wanted to see the oldest city of East Africa. Earlier the slave ships from the Congo came into this port. Their sad cargo was driven into a great courtyard and sold to those who had come there to buy. In this fateful city there was no longer any possibility of flight; their misery was final. The name Bagamayo indicates this, for it means literally: "Crush your heart—for all is lost now."

Today the city is a nest of filth with miserable, half-ruined houses and the usual handicraft shops on the street. Unexpectedly, between ruins and slums there are traces of the long, lost greatness —some splendidly carved beams, perhaps, or elegant heavy doors. Often they are hidden in back courtyards which we investigate —not only because of the remnants of the past, but also on account of the charming scenes which are offered there. Playing children, chanting mothers, fountains where people not only get water but also have fun. We gain entrance to these areas by giving the children candy. (We also gain the friendliness of the mothers.) Like the Pied Piper of Hamelin, we end up leading a great horde of children behind us. Since I am very good at making funny faces and they like to laugh, we are soon good friends and we also manage to get the somewhat reserved and often quite unfriendly looking men to accept us.

Thoroughly Muslim settlements such as this are often very backward and neglected. "Mohammedanism means hostility to progress," an expert on this country said to me recently. "Pay attention, and you can tell from the condition of the streets and houses what the religion is here." It might seem that such a sharply formulated and simplified rule would be teeming with exceptions. In Bagamayo, however, one tends to find this judgment confirmed.

At the edge of a side street a Koran school is being conducted out of doors. In front, with a gigantic book before him, sits a dignified looking old teacher. In front of him is a great crowd of men sitting on the ground in neat rows; a respectful distance behind them, women and girls. When we try to slip by as unobtrusively as possible they glance at us only fleetingly.

Directly upon the beach rises a fortress-like palace, the earlier residence of the German governor. Now it serves the district commissar as his residence and office. On the outer walls surrounding the park are bronze tablets with the names of fallen German colonial troops. We find it very peculiar in this distant place to find traces of German history—a history which recalls my earliest youth to me. An uncle of mine who was here often told of his days with the colonial garrison. Of the present day inhabitants no one is here. But a very friendly policeman, a gigantic man who is solemnly pacing outside, takes us immediately into the private rooms which are open. They too, with their magnificence and some furniture that remains, betray the traces of previous greatness. Like all administration and functional buildings from the German time, this residence has thick, solidly constructed stone walls which hold out the heat and outlast the times. From the great terrace one looks out past the park to the expanse of the ocean. I cannot resist casting a discreet glance at the bookshelf. In addition to many volumes of Marx and Lenin, I see there also a row of current German pocketbooks. The earlier time seems also to exert a linguistic influence. We chat with the policeman (who speaks English) about the years when the country was a German colony. When we, whose land resounds with permanent self-accusation and where it is almost a matter of good taste to defame our past, now hear something good about the colonial time, we almost feel like weeping!

In the courtyard of the palace two men incessantly turn the great wheels of a well; here there is no such thing as electric current. Immediately in the vicinity of the beach a giant tree towers. From its outstretched limbs those condemned to death were strung up. Now children play in its shadow. Further out we also enter a courtyard surrounded by houses and walls. Here the newly arrived slaves were driven together and suffered the nadir of their fate. Now grass grows through the cracks in the wall. Children run about, and this former place of hopelessness now becomes a point of reference for idyllic feelings, a disgraceful romanticism we strive to throw off. History buries the worst and the greatest in the bottomless abyss of the past and almost makes fantasy of it. Suddenly in this formerly sad but now cheerful spot a thought revives in me which I first had in the face of the fresh destruction and ruins of the war: while the first whirring dust blew out of them I thought how only yesterday they were homes and those now buried in them slept in them and sat around the lamp in the evening. One yet smelled the scent of fresh destruction, the smell of burned wood and the suffocating mixture of ashes and water from the firehoses. Soon, however, I said to myself at that time, new houses will stand upon this place, and the pile of rubbish will wear a mantle of green. No one will then be able to comprehend how we may stand, shaken, in the middle of these ruins or what fears reach out to us.

While strolling through side streets we discover the extremely simple workshop of a silversmith, whom we watch. With his unusually sensitive, finely nerved hands he does filigree work which we must use a magnifying glass to appreciate. Working with a type of oxygen blower, he solders together tiny silver wires for his fine Arabian web. The blower is a tiny train oil lamp in which he violently blows the flame at the little silver wires through a curved pipe. When we wish to buy something from him we can only make ourselves understood through a neighbor who has been called in to translate his Arabian into English. He cannot write or read numbers when I hold out a slip of paper and a ball point pen to him. And yet this man, whose features are not unintellectual and possess a strange melancholy charm, makes silver forms of indescribable delicacy and precision.

Before we begin the journey home we visit a Catholic mission on the edge of the city. The great, well-cared-for complex of buildings is dominated by a neo-romanesque, but all the same very dignified, cathedral which starkly contrasts with the decayed city. The entire structure has the effect of a rock in the middle of a sea of Mohammedanism. The isolated priest who administers his office here is a cheerful Dutchman. He does not betray in his bearing what it must mean for him to be surrounded by this strange and often hostile environment. His congregation of about one thousand is widely scattered. They, too, assert their existence only with difficulty. The Muslim world has long resisted all Christian missionary activity. On the walls of the little mission museum are many deeply impressive letters of emancipation in the German language and signed by German authorities.

As we finally drive homeward an evening peace is lying upon the settlements we pass. In lone huts we see small lights; the evening meal is being warmed upon coals. Occasionally music from loudspeakers reaches us. This evening it is mostly Christmas carols.

A swim on the beach of Mjimwema
Feeding a Python

Dar es Salaam
Sunday, December 27

Today the captain, the chief's family, our little mess steward Ernst, and we were invited to go swimming at an isolated beach by the German medical superintendent of the gynecological clinic here, Dr. Schuppler. We picked him up at his beautiful house which was built during the "German period." He has that vital dynamism and freshness one often finds among surgeons and obstetricians. He tells us with pleasure that on the first day of Christmas he brought fifty-three babies into the world in his clinic and that there are about 15,000 births per year. The expectant mothers come in the evening and leave on the bus the next morning, or they appear in the morning and leave the clinic on the evening of the same day. "Only in this way can we manage this great number," he says. "Embolism and much else which threatens the civilized women in Europe are scarcely known here. That our women here get up immediately afterwards and move about is healthy and prevents many complications." When we express our surprise that he does not lock his house when he leaves and ask him if he doesn't fear thieves—we have already heard of this bane here—he tells us laughingly that he has never encountered this problem. "I owe it to a trick I thought up. You see, I spread the rumor that every night a ghost rises up out of a dark corner of the great terrace and changes from a wispy smoke into a shape. To support this rumor I showed my servants a series of photos in which this ghost is to be seen. The rumors spread like wildfire and protect my house better than dogs, snakes, and a hyena, all of which I also have by the way."

At the splendid beach at Mjimwema which extends infinitely and is almost without people—if only we had something like this at home!—we rent a couple of reed huts and give ourselves over to creaturely comfort for the entire day. Mrs. Sch. provides us with good things to eat, as does the captain, for whom the steward has richly provided.

Coming home, Dr. Sch. insists on visiting his python which lived with him a long time as a house pet, until it got too large. Now it is, so to speak, in puberty and measures four meters long. In maturity it is supposed to grow to twice that length. It "resides as a guest" at a Catholic mission and remains, in spite of all the intimate coaxing sounds its master whispers through the wire meshing, all rolled up within itself and unmoved. Every month it eats a chicken. Since it is again time for this feeding, the keeper wants us to witness it. When he catches a chicken, the ladies protest and lament the poor innocent victim. "But the snake must also live!" says the keeper, unconsciously making reference to the conflict which rules nature. "Besides," he continues, "you don't need to worry about the chicken. It happens so fast it scarcely notices anything." And when one of us reaches for a camera he warns: "That has never succeeded! You would have to have a slow-motion apparatus in order to catch this lightning-like occurrence." He then lets the chicken flutter down into the snake's cage. The word lightning was really precise: we did not even see the snake rise up. We only saw the chicken surrounded by the snake in the next instant, crushed, and giving forth only small twitching movements.

"Death occurs," says Dr. Sch., "when the snake's lightning-fast contraction presses all of the blood into the skull of the chicken and bursts the veins. Thus the chicken is immediately stunned. In spite of this suffocating embrace the python does not break a single bone of the chicken." We now watch fascinatedly to see what will occur. Only after about twenty minutes, in which nothing at all happens, does the snake begin carefully to move about and probe all around with its head. It is obviously insuring the greatest security. For when it begins to swallow the chicken it is completely defenseless for an hour. With its overfull and distended mouth it is at the mercy of any enemy. Then it begins slowly to swallow the chicken with all its feathers. At first it is incomprehensible how the small head is to handle the chicken, which is several times larger. But the jaws are connected with elastic bands and finally accomplish the improbable task. "What does it do with all the feathers and bones?" asks little Sprat. "Surely it can't digest them!"

"Oh, yes it can, and very easily," says the keeper. "Nothing will be left of all that. It finally eliminates only a couple of quills. And those we sell for the mission," he adds, smiling. In the evening our swimming and snake club goes on board for supper and some final chatting. The Jahnels also join us. We are celebrating our farewell to Dar es Salaam, for tomorrow we are to leave.

Questionable developmental aid from the church

Pastor J. seems not at all exhausted after the superabundance of services he has absolved in the last three days. When I notice he is a little depressed and mention it to him, he says it has nothing to do with being tired, but that he is only thinking of the lack of developmental aid for the church. "Look, we needed a modest little community center in———[I have forgotten the name] to act as a focal point for the scattered Christians, to instruct them and give them tips in hygiene, agriculture, and other things. But over and over again we are refused it. On the 'spiritual front' we have been totally abandoned. If we ask for a hospital or school, the money is immediately forthcoming. But for a church or a center for the congregation, you can write until your fingers ache and beg until your throat is hoarse. For this there is only now and then a scanty dribble of money."

Dr. Sch., at whom he has glanced as he says this, smiles: "I understand you very well. I know they have nothing at all against hospitals and schools!"

"So do I!" Pastor J. says, grinning, but then becomes suddenly serious again. "No one doubts how necessary genuine aid is, or that one must fight illiteracy, or how important it is to provide for artificial fertilization and to give aid to the undernourished. But isn't that the task of *state* developmental aid? If we as the church are only a smaller version of the state and forget our special commission, we are lost and sold out."

"And what do you see as this special commission?" asks Mrs. Sch.

"Above all," continues the pastor, "that we protect the spiritual foundation which has been entrusted to us. We must proclaim and show man how he is to be redeemed from the dreadful fetters in which he is entangled. We see and experience this daily. And it makes a great difference whether one sees this from the outside as a theologian, or is directly involved in the fear and cursing hate and horrors of magic as a minister. We must seek these lost souls and bring them that freedom in which we ourselves live. One is not to be obtained without the other. The person who merely proclaims and works for the souls without thinking of the suffering of the undernourished bodies, is just as guilty as someone who says, "If one takes care of food, drink, clothing, and a place to live, one has done everything necessary for life." Pastor J. looks at me. His glance seems to ask whether I agree with him.

"I agree with everything you have said," I answer him. "During the Enlightenment, theologians thought that the gospel as a message which makes men free was superfluous and to be replaced with what we today call 'social ethics': moralistic philippics are now given from the pulpit concerning hygienic questions, good stable fertilizer, clean air in the bedroom, neatness in house and garden, and peaceful family life. It had been correctly perceived that the gospel also influenced these areas and changed life—simply because wherever it is really received it absolutely revolutionizes everything. But that element which you previously called 'the spiritual foundation' was forgotten. The gospel was permitted to degenerate into a mere therapy for symptoms, and it was forgotten that it seizes the *roots* of our existence, that it above all makes new *men* of us. In place of 'the one thing which is necessary' were substituted the many things which can be useful. And, indeed, we saw that this entire ten-

192

dency was deathly, that people were being spiritually starved and were fed instead of the bread of life the stones of moralism. When today faith is changed to mere good fellowship and theology to sociology, I see in it precisely the same form of degeneration and of spiritual death. The church then fails in its proper duty and gives men nothing other than what the welfare and socialistic states give them—and give them more efficiently. After a while people will say: 'If I can get what the church advertises just as easily from the secular society, *without* the Christian trappings, then I snap my fingers at the Christian trappings. At any rate, the church has become foreign to me (because the church itself no longer seems to have any interest in explaining its relevance to me).' When the church no longer provides what is most proper to it, what distinguishes it from everything men are able to provide, then it has betrayed itself and sold out. The short transitional phase when the so-called progressives celebrate the church and flatteringly endorse it, saying that it is moving with the times and is finally effecting a 'practical' Christianity—this short in-between stage will quickly pass."

What does "Love thy neighbor" mean?

"Do you mean," objects Dr. Sch. questioningly, "that the church should, in general, give up all programs such as practical aid in hygiene, agriculture, and animal husbandry and devote itself only to the care of souls?"

"By no means," I answer. "And Pastor J. didn't mean that either. It depends only upon the degree of urgency with which they are administered along with the mission of the church . . ."

"And that can only mean," adds Pastor J., "that the spiritual foundation occupies the prime position in our mission. We cannot concern ourselves with the branches and forget the roots."

I extend his line of thought and am glad of our agreement: "If one understands that Christian love is not only private charity and the merciful binding up of wounds; if one, rather, is aware that he also must prevent wounds and that this is only to be achieved by the revision of the social structure, then, naturally, all of this is part of our commission as a Christian community. But how are we to fulfill this commission? We cannot and should not do it directly. Rather *here* we should call upon the state—above all *our* state—and indicate to it its duty to give aid. It is, so to speak, the watchdog function of the church to work for the public good, to expose extremes of prosperity, and to appeal for aid for underdeveloped nations."

"Haven't you just expressed a condemnation of our mission hospitals?" asks Dr. Sch. again. "They are, of course, supported by the Christian community, although, according to your conception, they would have to fall into the category of *state* aid— or have I understood you incorrectly?"

"He scarcely meant it in that way," answers Pastor J. instead of me. "Care of the sick and care for souls are inextricably intertwined in medical aid. Thus we also have 'denominational' hospitals at home. But even in the other kind of hospital, the pastor, as a rule, has a place."

A further argument occurs to me: "Completely aside from this connection between medical aid and 'service to the inner man,' I would consider the purpose of a mission hospital here in Tanzania justified if it simply were aimed only at helping and—as in Dr. Walther's case—training the natives for medical self-help. Naturally it could be asked, as Dr. Sch. has just indicated, whether this duty did not fall into the jurisdiction of *state* medical care. Perhaps it does. What happens, however, if the state does *not* recognize this or does not *yet* recognize it? This is, after all, a developing country which is just beginning to awaken and look

194

around! I believe there is something like an emergency substitution by the church in the area of state jurisdiction. Here Christians who are living in a more advanced stage of history will discover a service to humanity which must be done and which the others cannot yet do, or perhaps do not even see. In this instance it behooves a Christian community to intervene in the name of love. Dr. Walther would certainly be glad if the education of his medical aids were seen as a model which then would be taken up by the state welfare agencies and continued on a large scale. The missionaries did something quite similar when they not only preached but also instructed the women in sewing and child care and the men in reading, writing, and agriculture. That, too, was and is an emergency substitution related to the message of love. And the mission cannot have intended to maintain a monopoly for the future in agricultural and other instruction."

After this somewhat strenuous debate on first principles, the conversation passes over into an easy banter. The presence of an experienced doctor so knowledgeable in the life of the country leads me to ask him once again about various things which are as yet unclear to me. I am interested in what he will say of my impression that the Africans here at the harbor are so especially lazy. When I describe to him very graphically what I saw in the way of organized laziness during the loading operations, it causes the others to laugh. "But I still don't trust the opinion, widespread on our ship, that this indolence, which is especially striking in comparison with Mozambique, is to be traced merely to differences of political system—here socialistic authoritarian, there capitalistic and competitive."

"This distrust is fairly justified," answers Dr. Sch. "But at any rate that is certainly not the only reason. The people are all slightly undernourished and, most importantly, have an unbalanced diet. Thus they are not particularly agile, especially in this humid heat. One must be aware of the fact that the dock workers on an average earn 150 schillings per month; that is to say, 75 German marks, and with that must try to feed two wives and their children. You can imagine then what kind of diet they have."

Naturally one could ask now if the poor wages themselves were not the result of the system. But however that may be, I'm glad I asked. Things now look a little different than before—to all of us. And tomorrow and the day after tomorrow and in the next year when I am again here, they will probably again present themselves in a different light. Where, then, lies the truth, and how does one get to it? Africa is full of enigmas.

At sea
On the way to Tanga
December 28

We have just left Dar es Salaam. At the outermost harbor exit stand Dr. Sch. and his wife, who was such an enlivening element during the fun of swimming and socializing. They wave with large white handkerchiefs and our fog horn drones three greetings back to them. And soon they disappear from our view.

In Tanga

Tanga
December 29

I believe I got a slight sunstroke on the beach at Mjimwema. At any rate I have a temperature, chills, and feel dizzy. But the 50-kilometer drive to Pangani on which we were invited along with the captain, was something I did not want to miss. Of course, I saw everything as if through a fog.

Our ship lies far out at anchor. The trip in the boat across the picturesque bay to shore was very pretty, and the way through the neat city, with its broad avenues of mangos and modest but tasteful and solid houses, gives a Germanic impression and reminds us of Hermann von Wissmann's work. We drive on tidy though unasphalted streets through the largest area of sisal cultivation in the world. In the nineties of the previous century Richard Hindorf brought the sisal root here from Mexico and thereby established the basis for an export business which is now threatened by competition from the synthetic fiber industry. We encounter the little settlement of Kikombe which makes a striking impression from the road because the outside walls of the houses are painted with colorful scenes. Our driver, however, for unfathomable reasons, cannot be persuaded to show us what is behind these façades. With obvious nervousness he insists upon driving on immediately and not allowing us to get out. I have already noticed several times a certain embarrassment with our native drivers in their attempts to prevent us from seeing one thing or another. Perhaps this time, too, there are personal reasons. At any rate we respect them and drive on. At Pangani we have the feeling of being at the end of the world. We think we see evidence in the aloof and somewhat curiously staring faces of the Moslem inhabitants that Europeans seldom come here. The only whites in the village are an English couple, he a former major, she a charming, wizened old lady. The two have been operating here for decades a workshop which in originality has no peer. With very little machinery, mostly by hand, they produce the most varied things: chairs, armchairs, boats, toys, and much else. The most interesting thing to me is a sewing machine which has been built solely of bicycle parts. It is suited to the natives' simple modes of work and can also be easily repaired because the necessary screws, chains, and wheels can be obtained in any bicycle shop. The entire business looks as if the two old people had said good-by to the civilized world in order to devote themselves to the hobby and handicraft work which help the natives improve their life. Here, like Robinson Crusoe, they are building simple things with knowledge from the civilized world.

Pangani itself is a dirty little place distinguished only by a few buildings from the German period. These have to some degree withstood the lack of any maintenance. One sees nothing— at least we didn't—of the early Arabian history of this village or of the fact that it was probably already playing a role in the first century. What most especially impresses me in my somewhat foggy condition is a Moslem patriarch who walks about in erect and almost solemn dignity surrounded by three wives and numerous children who accompany him in silent respect.

Kenya

In Mombasa; conversations on the Indian Ocean

Since yesterday I have been down in bed. My temperature has risen considerably, and I am alternately hot and cold, as if my inner thermostat were defective. As far as I have been able to learn from the doctor, it is a cross between the flu and sunstroke. Last night I had a maddening thirst and searched through the entire ship to find something to drink. In thoughts and images of my fever I was obsessed again by the deep and gigantic crisis of the university. Idea: if there were equality and leveling everywhere, the chances of the stronger and more intelligent would be decreased because they would have to deal with and be dependent upon all the small minds which would have the majority voice. They cannot succeed in gaining a ground upon which they can operate with security—I believe this was an echo of my readings in Churchill's *Marlborough,* where he describes the different circumstances of the eighteenth century. But that, too, was no Paradise!

After days muddled by fever, today, for the first time, I am almost without temperature and noticeably stronger. In spite of my befogged condition, Mr. B., the general agent of our line for East Africa, took us for the duration of our stay in Mombasa to the white dream villa of Mrs. von Rantzau far out of the city on the sea. "There we shall take care of you until you are well."

The phrase "white dream villa" unpleasantly reminds me, of course, of the "jasmine and rainbow" style. But no other description seems to fit. It is really white and is really a large villa with broad terraces and great columns. And before it is a parklike garden with a swimming pool. This garden runs down to the beach, so that I hope soon to do what the others are doing: get out of bed in the morning, run down to the sea, and then wash off the salt water in the swimming pool. Five helpful servants see to our wishes, among them a cook with a great cap who after every meal appears before his public like a symphony conductor to receive applause. Mr. B. is still unmarried, a young, radiant, energy-charged man with whom one immediately feels comfortable. But being alone in this great house with the horde of black servants is, in spite of its fairytale atmosphere, often a burden to him. He is glad we are visiting him. And not only we: the German ambassador in Kenya had written me a very nice letter and has sent two young theologians from Nairobi to "entertain" me—Father Sp. of the White Fathers and the Protestants' pastor, H. The two are close friends, work together and even publish their own journal, the quality of which is impressive. They are just as disappointed as we that my silly illness prevents us from realizing the alluring plans they have made for us: since the priest is also a pilot, a "flying priest," they planned for us to fly in a small charter plane through Kenya to isolated caravans in the desert with which the priest is in contact. So here I sit in a lovely villa in Kenya which has so totally filled my imagination since reading Robert Ruark's book *Uhuru*. Right before my nose is the possibility for a very unusual adventure—but I must play the wretched part of the semi-invalid.

I was not yet able to celebrate New Year's although the evening on the terrace by the sea certainly was very beautiful. But since yesterday we have been talking the entire time with our two visitors and are trying to find out as much as possible about their work and about Kenya.

Does the mission lead the African to self-estrangement?

Father Sp. also sees the African mission in a crisis. He speaks of the end of a former conception and regards the new one which is already evident in its outlines with great concern. He says: "The political and ecclesiastical independence of Africa no longer permits evangelical orders which commit their members to a lifetime of work in Africa. Our work will experience a development similar to that seen in the realms of government and economy: we must provide advisors for a limited length of time, say, for six years. That can be fruitful and useful for everyone. Otherwise we will never wean the Africans, will prevent independent development, and cause Christianity to remain forever basically a foreign import."

To my question as to his relationships with his African colleagues, his straightforward answer, which is characteristic of all his expression, immediately instills in me a sense of trust: "There remains between us and our black brothers a barrier. Not to recognize this would be self-delusion that would lead to hypocrisy. Precisely because I recognize the fact that they are different I have come to the conclusion we must step into the background and limit ourselves to the role of mere advisors. When the barrier between us completely drops—that happens sometimes—it is as a rule *not* a good sign. Then the African has adopted a European style of life and is estranged from himself and his tribal brothers. And this, especially, we do *not* want."

Wishing to provoke him a little, I ask: "Couldn't this estrangement, on the whole, be the result of mission work?"

"Only when mission work is carried out 'according to the book,' " he answers, "when, for example, we simply dictate our songs, our ceremonies and institutions to the Africans. This actually leads them to estrangement. Besides, it shows a lack of faith: one does not count on the creative power of faith to show our African brothers their own way and their own style."

I don't quite know whether it is an objection or only an extension when I say to the father that I would go still further: "I for my part also consider it 'according to the book' when we present certain *ethical* ideas of our Christian tradition as essentially Christian and demand the same recognition for them as, for instance, for the idea that Christ is the Lord."

"Do you have something special in mind?" asks the father.

"Yes. To us, for example, monogamy is *the* Christian form of marriage. This has its justification, of course, and I do not wish to argue against it. Monogamy is related to a change in the position of woman which Christianity brings. I thus believe it will be in force everywhere under the influence of Christianity. I consider it 'according to the book' and thus counterproductive, however, when certain missionaries say: God requires monogamy of you. Before you can be baptized you must give up all your wives except one. I consider this extremely un-Christian; here there is not the patience to allow a certain way of life to *grow* as the fruit of the gospel. Instead, this way of life is put before the gospel and made a precondition for accepting it. This is a perfect example of doing things according to the book. Besides, I consider such behavior un-Christian also because it is highly uncharitable, even hideous, when nothing less is required than, for instance, for a chief to dissolve a relationship of trust with one or more of his wives and—in the present circumstances!—relegate them to a life without identity or to prostitution. He will probably choose the youngest and freshest and let the old ones look out for themselves. Here, too, as you quite correctly have

202

said, one does not trust anything to the creative power of faith; that by the force of its influence—perhaps in the next generation —it will bring about monogamy."

The priest does not enter into this discussion, perhaps because his ecclesiastical obligations make this theme a delicate one. I do not consider it impossible, however, that he agrees with me. Instead, he once again takes up the subject of the false Europeanization of the African as it comes about by organizing a mission "according to the book."

He tells of a recently experienced instance which greatly appalled him: "The rector of a theological school in Nairobi asked one of the African students: 'What do you see as the goal of your work when you return to the bush?' Answer: 'Who wants to go back to the bush again!' Somewhat bitterly the priest adds: 'The young man simply thought, that's what the white people do! They are suitable for the bush.'

"Some time ago it was a similar matter at a Corpus Christi procession. Things like this appeal to the African proclivity for the theatrical and thus are very well received by the people. The students, however, refused to participate. After they had at first tried to excuse themselves on various pretexts, they finally came to the real reason: 'It is too hot. We cannot stand in the sun so long.' Really and truly that is what they said: 'We cannot stand in the sun so long.'" He shakes his head. "There you have the whole estrangement our misdirected education produces," he continues somewhat excitedly. "The status of a cleric, according to our American or European model, brings him unbelievable social prestige in the African society and removes him from his old environment. You should just hear and see what all this 'cleric' may no more do and what he owes to his position! This is, however, not the result of the gospel, but the result of its misuse. Instead of the gospel, we have imported a European Christianity and are then surprised that, in spite of all outer acceptance, it remains foreign and in addition leads to alienation and estrangement."

Pastor H. enlarges upon this theme by relating a scandal I had previously heard about: a Protestant bishop, an African—who had, by the way, even studied under me in Hamburg—had, in spite of the poverty of his church, bought an expensive large automobile which costs about twice as much here as in Germany. He had also otherwise run up such expenses that he literally bankrupted his poor church. He had to resign after a short time. (People told me about this in almost every port.) "The bishop, in all honesty, did not consider himself a swindler, although he knew quite well that things had to collapse," adds Pastor H., who knows him. "He said, in all naïveté, that an ecclesiastical figure like himself was obligated to his position, and that besides, he was also the son of a chief. Here African ideas about prestige were frightfully mixed with exaggerated notions about European dignity."

Today I too finally begin the day with an early dip in the salt and fresh waters. After breakfast we meet in the garden and, sitting under the palms, continue the conversation of yesterday. I comment that Pastor J. complained about church developmental aid and asked me whether the same difficulties existed in the Catholic church. Father Sp. confirms that in his church too absolutely anything can be obtained for concrete developmental projects, but that for the expenses of the missionaries, that is, for work "in spiritual matters," only the bare necessities were provided. Through agreements with the native bishops the daily pay for a missionary was set at from three to at most five schillings (from 75 cents to a dollar). Of course, one could not live on that, even with the most modest requirements. Thus support had to come from relatives. In general, relations with the native episcopacy were not without tensions. It is hyperconservative and opposes the ideas of the younger men of whom we had spoken yesterday. The style of rule is in many ways like that of tribal chiefs. Nearly all the younger people suffer from the fact that free expression of opinions is scarcely permitted.

When what is gradually revealed in the course of a long conversation is written down in such a concentrated fashion it would almost seem as if the father had become querulous. This was by no means the case and he himself is never like this. He is filled with the joy of his service, and all criticism—all perhaps revolutionary attitudes—cannot smother the enthusiasm with which he is devoted to it. Neither can they obscure his sober but deep goodness. What gives me the most joy is the straightforwardness which makes it impossible for him to attempt to give a retouched picture to the representative of another denomination. The fact that he gives his ideas so openly is probably made easier by his close relationship with the pastor. In him he has a good comrade who bears similar burdens and not only sees the same goals but also struggles with him to reach them.

Celibacy among African priests

When I tease the priest a little for being a clerical revolutionary —our conversation was not carried on in a terribly serious manner, especially not in this fairytale milieu! I mention my Catholic friends in Holland who, since the Council, are especially hostile about the question of celibacy and are pressing for radical reforms. I can imagine that this problem is especially delicate in this country. An unmarried African—that is almost unthinkable; in fact, it seems an almost unreal abstraction. Does the "sexual" temper of the African make a celibate existence at all possible? I ask this question as if I were talking to myself. I would like to give the father an opportunity not to take it up in case the question, which could only be answered with one's own experiences, should seem too indiscreet to him. But here, too, he enters into the subject in his frank manner:

205

"The question of celibacy, indeed, causes us a great deal of difficulty with the young African theologians. Of the approximately eighty students of an East African seminary, thirty withdrew in the last year because they were not able to take this vow. I spoke with all of them and had to respect their motives. They were the very best. They rejected the 'Italian solution' by which celibacy as an institution remains untouched but relief is sought through 'private solutions.' They would have preferred an institutional honesty. But this is not to be attained at the moment."

"Isn't there perhaps another difficulty," I ask him now somewhat more directly, "that celibacy under certain circumstances is a greater burden for the black man than for the white?"

The priest confirms this and refers to the fact that the sexual drive of the African, on account of physiological requirements, is in general doubtlessly stronger than that of the "European." The father then adds a remark which, surprisingly, agrees with certain opinions I have repeatedly expressed in discussions with my students. He says: "In Europe sex has been crushed down by removing the aura of taboo from it. The constant confrontation with it in illustrated magazines, films, and in otherwise ubiquitous pornographic publications, the constant public talking about it, and the permanent loosening of inhibitions, allows its force to escape through countless valves and weakens its elemental power. Here in Africa, however, it rules in uninterrupted vehemence." I seem to sense that the father is thinking about a Catholic priesthood that can be completely fulfilled without celibacy. Now I become bold: I play the devil's advocate and, as a Protestant, break a lance for celibacy. How will the priest react to this? I say to him: "I understand very well that the Vatican would disturb the institution of celibacy only with the greatest reluctance. I believe this structure has a decisive part in what one considers the strength and the energy of the Roman Catholic church. During his dictatorship Hitler hesitated for a long time to risk an argument with the Catholic church because he considered this 'society of men' invincible; it is bound not to wife and child but only to its vows. I am also thinking of how much harder it is, for instance, for a pastor with his family in areas influenced by Communism. In addition to the responsibility for his congregation, he also bears a heavy responsibility for his children, whom he must protect from the attacks of ideological atheism and whom he would like to see educated in freedom. This conflict of responsibilities brings him into disaccord—often into a debilitating inner conflict!—which the Roman priest at least is spared and which therefore does not inhibit his service. Don't you also think that one should give up this energy potential only with reluctance?"

The father agrees, even though he wonders—I had only intended to entice him out of his shell!—that I of all people should say that. For, he says, I must certainly know that a married pastor also has *positive* qualifications for service. One need only remember the role of the pastor's house in German cultural history. This is something which I myself cannot and will not contradict. But I am waiting to see what further critical points the father has to make in spite of the decisive argument he has just accepted. Neither is he for radical revolutionary solutions. He is, as stated, even prepared to accept my idea that celibacy represents an enormous potential for the energy of his church. But he will admit this only under one condition: that the *pragmatic* character of this point of view is straightforwardly admitted and that celibacy is no longer justified—as is often the case today!—with questionable, windy, and far-fetched arguments taken from the arsenal of dogma and Holy Script. In the name of truth this cannot be permitted. And since celibacy has *no* "dogmatic" status, it cannot be made universally obligatory. If that were to be done, it would not only be a sin against the truth but would place a yoke on countless others which they would be unable to bear. It would force them rather to commit hypocrisy and cause them to go about with a bad conscience. Therefore, he suggests *voluntary*

207

celibacy. It should, for this reason, never come to the point that—as with Protestantism—marriage is *expected* of priests. It should only be *possible* in addition to celibacy.

I am very moved by the fact that the same problems which cause us to hold our breath in Europe also charge the atmosphere here "at the end of the world." It makes an impression upon me to hear them presented not by a theological observer but by a man who stands in the middle of the battle. He has devoted his life to such problems and, in spite of all critical earnestness, looks full of confidence into a future which, although hidden from our view, is guided by another.

Our morning conversation is concluded with a lunch taken on the terrace of the English Club immediately next to "Fort Jesus." Then the two friends leave for Nairobi. "We want to be there before dark," they say. "It is unpleasant when a zebra jumps in front of the headlights or an elephant blocks the way at night."

Now, on account of my stupid fever, I have seen almost nothing of Kenya. Afternoon explorations of Mombasa are no substitute. But my two guests have richly recompensed me with their stories and discussions. But when I think that I had almost flown with them to the caravans in the desert and spent the nights under a nomad tent . . .

Almost dishonest fishing

Mombasa
The last day in Africa
January 3

Today we leave. But before we go back to the ship there is a fishing excursion on a charter boat under the direction of two native fishermen. Mr. B. has invited us along.

We start out early. The little boat bounces quite a bit in the violent movement of the sea during the five-hour cruise. Cunningly, we trawl four long lines with bait. We enjoy watching the skillful hands of the Africans as they merrily attach the minnows. During the cruise they seem to flit through the water like living animals (except on somewhat too straight a course!). Even after we had already been under way for three hours, no creature of the deep had considered biting, so finally I fall asleep in my swivel chair. Suddenly I am awakened by loud cries in German, Kikuyu, and English. "A bite. We have one!" And quickly someone presses the successful fishing rod into my hand. With heart pounding with fear and excitement, I bring the catch on board with alternate slacking and pulling on the rod and simultaneously rolling of the line. It is hot and difficult work: the fish must really be a big one. Finally, finally, the fishermen —not I!—pull him on deck with a skillful swing: a great splendid silver fish which wriggles pitifully and makes me feel somewhat sorry. Now they give me exaggerated congratulations and act as if I had made this brilliant catch by shrewd searching out of a likely place, skillful manipulation, and a watchfulness which nothing escapes. In truth, however, I had dozed off and they had pressed the baited rod with the fish into my hand while I was still half asleep. When I see this hypocrisy I suppress an ironic laugh (which the good people probably think is a howl of joy over "my" success). I seem to myself like an old emperor on the hunt. The game was so driven before the senile old man that no one besides him would be able to miss it. When the accompanying forester pulled his trigger in good synchronization his serene highness considered himself to be a successful hunter. When now the customary flag is raised on one of the fishing rods, announcing the successful catch to everyone and we tie up under the curious eyes of onlookers, I am almost ready to believe myself a child of good fortune upon whose head the blessing of Saint Peter had descended in complete justification.

To stretch our legs we stroll a little through the city, where the stores are open in spite of the fact that it is Sunday and an endless stream of people moves through the streets. There is no talk here of the desolation of the city! A great, brand-new building complex is covered with flags. It is the new main post office which is to be presented in the morning by the president. The port and mercantile city of Mombasa makes a much more prosperous and metropolitan impression than the other cities of East Africa we have seen. The harbor traffic is also very much better organized. As we have been told, President Kenyatta, whose patriarchal smiling face looks down from countless pictures, has placed many white advisors in key positions. Indeed, at the harbor one repeatedly meets Europeans who have special responsibilities.

Although Kenya is connected with Tanzania by a common currency and in many other ways, there is no question here of Chinese influence or of socialistic tendencies. We have seen no one here with a Mao bible. The country seems to have outgrown the labile uncertainty of Mau Mau and Uhuru times and to have consolidated. Steadily increasing its income by advertising itself as a vacation and safari paradise, it attracts great streams of tourists. Even the vacationers who come from America or Europe to go on to Tanzania for a safari are accustomed first to land in Nairobi.

Later we sit once again on the terrace for a last cup of tea. Once again we enjoy the roomy, comfortable house and the silent attentiveness of the boys. Once again our eyes look out over the palms to the shining blue sea. And yet somewhere inside of us there is a soft ticking sound which disturbs the complete enjoyment of these moments. It finally gains verbal form in the question—which drops somewhat heavily into the smoothly rippling teatime conversation—whether we can today enjoy all this with an untroubled mind. Isn't there something here from a time that is, in fact, already past? Will it not, in double quick march, take with it all that has been so dear to us in these days and has given us such pleasure? Shouldn't we snap ourselves back to reality when we begin to enjoy the anachronistic bliss of a dying style of life? Are we allowing the black people who surround us as such willing servants really to be what they are supposed to be? Aren't we here, yet again, playing the "white masters" which basically we are not at all, any more?

This hour of farewell is not suited to the burden of melancholy debates over basic principles. We are glad then when the young master of the house seeks to shoo away these creeping specters with a light hand. "Believe me," he emphasizes with great conviction, "these people feel wonderfully at home in this house. With the wink of an eye they often help me to understand that it is their nature to be contented, that they are happy to have this easy job which does well by them, and that they have, besides, enough time left over to have fun together. The cook is happy when guests come, and he can show what skills he knows. You have seen for yourselves with what beaming satisfaction he always receives the applause of those whom he has just fed." Although he is quite strict with them, they seem to love him. It is no secret to them that he has a heart for them and is concerned for their needs and those of their families. They are happy and laugh frequently. In our memories they are like the young fellows who stand around in cheerful groups on the street corners of Mombasa, or like those who observe from windows or balconies the eternally old and always new surging crowds in the streets. They do not yet know the melancholy of Europe.

When we arrive at the ship in the evening we are greeted as members of a family who have been away for a long time. The large tuna which I drag along and hand over to the cook for our dining table naturally stirs up a great hullabaloo. Now I am really convinced I caught it myself and allow myself to be toasted without blushing! Two English families have newly arrived on board. The hectic atmosphere which usually fills a ship before its departure and causes it to resemble a beehive is especially great this time. For now we are setting out on an uninterrupted journey of twenty-six days to Naples. We will see a bit of land in the distance only now and again, sometimes a ship and otherwise only sky and water. What we have experienced in the past weeks is like a confusing movie with an overabundance of images and long dialogues. I am glad for the opportunity to digest my experiences, to read and write, dream and ponder—but also for some parties with which to punctuate the monotonously flowing days like caesuras.

When the last rope binding us to Africa is untied and the ship slowly glides out into the evening, we stand for a long time on deck. Now what was so near to us and yet so far, for all its nearness, moves into the distance.

Destination Naples

At sea
January 4

Africa is already far away, but it is still much in our thoughts. I am reminded of Jacob Burckhardt, who, before the onrush of the megalomaniac and technical age, wanted once more to visit Italy to "get an eyeful of beauty" before it passed away. We, too, have occasionally seen the real original Africa—perhaps only an eyeful, but something, nevertheless. Here, too, other times are rushing in which will change everything. Where there is now wilderness or lonely huts, vacation paradises will flourish and hordes of people will be flown in from all points of the globe. Carefully preserved folklore will be presented to them as the old, original life. Where now the steppes extend themselves, mines and industries will cause the landscape to resemble that image which is all too familiar to us in old Europe. Unadulterated elements will become goods in short supply. But it would be unallow-

212

able pessimism and, above all, sentimental to see in these coming things merely an end and a destruction. Only one thing is certain, the ambiguity of all things human will also be a part of what presents itself as progress and promises to lead us out from the dark realms of misery and poverty. But whatever shall happen and whatever changes may come about, the vision of an Africa which will soon no longer exist has impressed itself irrevocably upon our minds. "What once was never returns again . . . ," and what we expect to be the final future is related to other dimensions.